To Gary
Christmas 1980
From Mr & Mrs Everitt.

Below: The B-29 Superfortress destined for the Imperial War Museum collection at Duxford finally made it to the UK on 1 March 1980, and is seen here on the taxiway at RAF Mildenhall before its onward flight to Duxford the next day.
Denis J. Calvert

1981

aircraft ILLUSTRATED annual

Edited by
Martin Horseman

LONDON

IAN ALLAN LTD

Contents

This picture: Spitfire at low level — an air show beat-up at something less than 20ft! *Gordon Bain*

First published 1980

ISBN 0 7110 1046 3

Published by Ian Allan Ltd, Shepperton, Surrey; and printed by Ian Allan Printing Ltd at their works at Coombelands in Runnymede, England

'Old One-Six Charlie' flies the Eagle

Martin Horseman

Above: USAF Military Airlift Command C-130 Hercules at RAF Mildenhall from where the 313th Tactical Airlift Group co-ordinates the operations of the aircraft assigned to Europe on temporary duty (TDY) from US-based units.
All photos by the Author

Established at flight level 180 (18,000ft) the C-130 settled into a steady cruise at 270 knots TAS, heading due west for the UK and a well-earned night-stop at Mildenhall. It was 21.30hrs local time and we had just passed over the Belgian border with the Federal Republic of Germany, about 20min out of Ramstein. Up front, in the rounded apex of the Hercules' panoramic flight deck, the aircraft commander Capt Pete Discenza and co-pilot Capt Dave Bowyer eased into the en-route routines of monitoring the array of unblinking instrumentation staring back at them, and of securing the sequence of ground station check-ins and clearances which would make for an orderly progress home. Perched on his elevated pedestal of a seat in the centre of the cockpit area, flight engineer SSgt Ken Phipps was busy with write-ups in the log while running his eye over the roof panel dials and switches, and the engine and other controls on the central console. In the well-lit corner office of the 'navigation dept' 1Lt David Wood consulted his stock in trade — maps and charts of the route and related airways, and checked the assembly of information presented by his collection of repeater and specialist counter/pointer-type instruments (drift/angle, true air speed, ground speed, altimeter, distance measuring equipment, horizontal situation indicator, etc, etc). Our course lay west towards Brussels then northwest to the Channel coast, out over the southern North Sea, and across East Anglia to Mildenhall — the centre of USAF tactical airlift operations based in the UK. It was the last leg of a round trip to Spain and back which is flown three times a week by Military Airlift Command C-130 Hercules crews assigned on temporary duty (TDY) with the 313th Tactical Airlift Group.

Code-named the *European Eagle* this scheduled service departs from Mildenhall every Monday, Wednesday and Friday and links the Suffolk base with Torrejon AB near Madrid, Spain via intervening stops at Ramstein AB, Germany and Aviano AB, Italy. Then on Tuesdays, Thursdays and Saturdays the *Eagle* aircraft and crew turn round at Torrejon and retrace their path back along the route to Mildenhall. With intermediate, 2hr stopovers and the 'big bird's' stately passage down the line, (average flying time, end-to-end, about 8 hrs), it may not be the world's fastest mode of personnel and freight transport but, as one of the crew remarked of the Hercules, 'this airplane sure gets the job done': and as our ship — a C-130E s/n 72-1293, with the homely sounding call sign

'Old 16 Charlie' — churned faithfully onwards, it did indeed seem custom-built for the task.

This particular MAC traverse of Central and Southern Europe had got underway some 40hrs previously as the outbound half of the double-header, Flight No 1717, was prepared on an early Monday morning at 'the Hall'. For Capt Discenza and his crew from the 50th Tactical Airlift Squadron of the 314th Tactical Airlift Wing at Little Rock AFB, Ark it was to be one of the concluding assignments during their 60-day tour in the UK, which has begun seven weeks before on 6 August 1979. Although the periods of TDY fulfilled in rotation by US-based C-130 squadrons are normally of 75 day duration, this detachment had been shorter — partly, it was thought, because of the greater call on the Stateside-based Hercules units now that the USAF C-141 modification programme is getting started (Lockheed is fitting a 23ft fuselage stretch and incorporating air refuelling receiver facilities into the 'A' model Starlifters to turn them into C-141Bs). So far as Hercules experience is concerned, we were to be in expert hands; the 50th TAS (known as the 'Red Devils') is one of the four squadrons in the 314th TAW — the USAF's C-130 training outfit. Pilot training is conducted by the Wing's 16th TATS and tactical training by the 62nd TAS, while the 50th and 61st TAS are attached as operational squadrons.

Reporting formalities completed at the Mildenhall MAC terminal, the flight was called shortly after 07.00hrs and the customers for '1717' boarded the bus for the Hercules' parking spot on the south side of the field — the aircraft would have been on the terminal ramp but for two C-5s and the presence of sundry C-141s crowding out the accommodation. With the loading quickly completed, the Herc's paddle-bladed Hamilton Standards were soon kaliedoscoping an accelerating pattern of shadow and thin dawn light through the few porthole-style windows in the cabin centre section. Away from the stand at 07.40hrs we taxied across the end of runway 11 for power checks on the north-side apron while a cell of KC-135s initiated their launch with a series of streamed take-offs. Then we were cleared, and at the appointed 08.00hrs departure time 'Old 16 Charlie' — 37 passengers; a crew of six (including two loadmasters) accompanied by three crew chiefs to tend to any away-from-base technical snags; 10,200lb of cargo; and 50,000lb of fuel — lifted its 145,000lb gross weight off the Mildenhall runway at 112kts and 15,500lb torque to become a blip on the Honington Zone controllers radar screens.

Earplugs fully in and fortified by a ready supply of coffee courtesy loadmasters MSgt Danny R. Hunter of our 50th TAS crew and SrA Matthew G. Tebbe of Mildenhall's 5th Mobile Aerial Port Squadron (whose loadmasters augment the Herc crews when there are more than 30 passengers on a flight), 1717's assorted complement of military and civilian travellers relaxed for the 1hr 35min sector to

Ramstein. This was the second time that the crew had flown the *Eagle* during their current TDY rotation. Up to that morning their deployment at Mildenhall had seen them amass about 140hr flying over Europe and with this round trip reckoned to add another 15-16hr, plus other tasks at the end of the week, they were expecting to total some 160hrs before returning to the US. It had been a fairly typical tour; other than the *Eagle* flights, the crew had been tasked on resupply sorties to installations in Turkey (the 'Turkey Trot' mission!) and general, 'off-the-wall trash-hauling', an all-embracing description of the Herc's ability to offer an as and when rostered, go-anyplace, and keep-on trucking style of freight service.

It is a way of life with which all C-130 crews quickly became familiar. In Capt Discenza's case, his assignment to the 50th TAS in January 1978 marked a re-acquaintance with the Lockheed-Georgia turboprop airlifter after four years as an instructor pilot on T-37s with USAF Air Training Command's 14th FTW at Columbus, Miss. Previously he had spent 15 months in SE Asia flying C-130s out of Taiwan. How did he find the flying over this side of the Atlantic? 'Well some of the pre-flight filing procedures are a little less than straightforward!' but he admitted that the crews 'are possibly rather spoiled back in the US' particularly in the flexibility they are accorded to depart from airways and proceed directly under their own navigation from point to point. In any event, they had not needed much time to become accustomed to operations in Europe as they had an RAF C-130 pilot on an exchange posting

Below: A C-130E Hercules, s/n 63-7891, on finals at Aviano AB, Italy, one of the transit points served by the *European Eagle*. The 'E' version of the Lockheed turboprop transport was the variant built in the largest numbers for the USAF, and it was a long-range development with provision for two 1,360 gal underwing fuel tanks and increased payload.

Above: Capts Pete Discenza, left, and Dave Boyer, right, at the controls of 'Old 16 Charlie' during the sector between Ramstein and Aviano.

with the squadron who had briefed them before their departure from Little Rock.

Soon it was time for the descent into Ramstein and after a glimpse on finals of the familiar sprawl of 'K-Town' (the city of Kaiserslautern) unwinding along the valley, 'Old 16 Charlie' alighted on the 86th Tactical Fighter Wing's 9,000ft of toned-down runway at the centre of the largest US air base in Europe. While the departing and transient passengers repaired to the MAC terminal from yet another ramp full of C-141s, C-130s and a C-5, the crew began preparations for the next stage, checked over the aircraft and shuffled the relevant cargo out of and into the hold. It was to be a relatively prompt turnaround: less than an hour after the 09.35hrs touchdown the passengers were boarding the coach for the trip out to the MAC ramp, and at 11.10hrs the *Eagle* was airborne again to head southeast from Ramstein across Southern Germany and over the Alps towards Italy.

On the 2hr 30min haul to Aviano there was plenty of time to look around the ship and pretty well everyone took advantage of the crew's hospitality on regular visits to the buffet. The latter formed part of the centrepiece store in the cargo hold — a freight container-like structure the creation of Brown Engineering and A. Teledyne Co, officially designated MCO-163A s/n 4N90000-101 and bearing its stencilled affiliation to Dover AFB, Del, the unit is universally referred to as a 'Comfort Pallet'. One half of the pallet was given over to a double rest room installation and 80gall capacity water tank, while on the opposite side was the buffet unit with three ovens, storage for 75 pre-prepared meals, and the much utilised coffee making facilities.

An hour or so into the flight the scenery down below was becoming progressively more spectacular as the Hercules flew onwards at FL 210 above the roof of Europe. The mountains in the Swiss and Austrian Alps were clear of cloud and several cameras were busy registering the breathtaking views for the folks back home.

And so 'downhill' into Aviano and yet another MAC terminal where we were to leave the aircraft for a 24hr stopover before picking up the return *Eagle* the following day. Flight 1717, meanwhile, continued on to Torrejon, arriving there at 20.30hrs to conclude a lengthy working day. The next morning the inbound mission to Mildenhall, tagged Flight No 1718, got off to another early start with the loading of the aircraft completed by 07.30hrs. Take-off

Above: The C-130E featured in this story, s/n 72-1293, lands at Ramstein on a rainy morning in August 1979 shortly after the start of its 60-day deployment to Europe.

Left: A sample of the view from the left side of 'Old 16 Charlie's' flight deck as the outbound Flight 1717 crossed the Alps at 21,000ft.

from the Spanish base was at 11.00hrs and some 2hr 45min later '1293' was down at Aviano for an almost equally long rest in the Italian sunshine of an autumn afternoon. Eventually the requisite clearances came through and 'Old 16 Charlie' was away at 16.20hrs with 37 passengers and 10,500lb of cargo — 9,000lb to be off-loaded at Ramstein and 1,500lb for onward delivery to Mildenhall. Ahead was the climb up and over the Alps and the early-evening to dusk trek northwest, watching — as in all good, big budget productions — the sun sinking slowly in the West! For the less tourist-minded other distractions were soon at hand in the form of a 'help yourself' box of snacks and soft drinks from the Comfort Pallet buffet. Presiding over the cabin activity MSgt Danny

Above: A C-130E Hercules flares for touchdown at Aviano, Italy — home of USAFE's 40th Tactical Group.

Hunter exuded the 'everything under control' — type approach appropriate to the 5,000hr MAC patch he wore. The greater part of his flight time as a loadmaster had been accumulated on C-124 Globemasters during 1966-69: a subsequent stint on the rather swifter Starlifter was followed by a five month tour in Vietnam, another period of duty with C-141s and then five years on C-130s, based latterly at Little Rock AFB, Ark since July 1977. While Danny attended to the miscellany of tasks which is the loadmaster's lot, SrA Matthew Tebbe was demonstrating to a regular flow of visitors that the buffet — like the Mobile Aerial Port Squadron motto *(Omnia, Semper, Ubique)* and maxim (5th MAPS 'Does It') — operates on an 'anything, anytime, anywhere' basis. Several cups of coffee afterwards and 2hrs out from Aviano we began the let-down into the Ramstein pattern, landing at 18.50hrs.

The cargo handling crew and equipment were upon the aircraft almost before the props had finished turning and a degree of hustle was in evidence to prevent the duration of the stopover and last leg to Mildenhall from turning the flight into another mission of 'Midnight Air Command', as MAC crews sometimes refer to their organisation's facility for round-the-clock operations. The crew chiefs spilled out to assist with the turn, the loadmasters 'so-longed' the departing passengers, and the flight crew headed for Base Ops to check the filing of the flight plan. An hour later the Herc was replete with a new complement of passengers and we were ready to go . . . or so we thought. As a delay became apparent, the aircraft commander was on the PA system to announce in best 'Captain speaking' manner that somewhere down the line from Base Ops to the German ATC network our flight plan had been mis-routed and that there would be a hold until the clearances were sorted out. Eventually a computer in the air traffic system rediscovered us and we set off

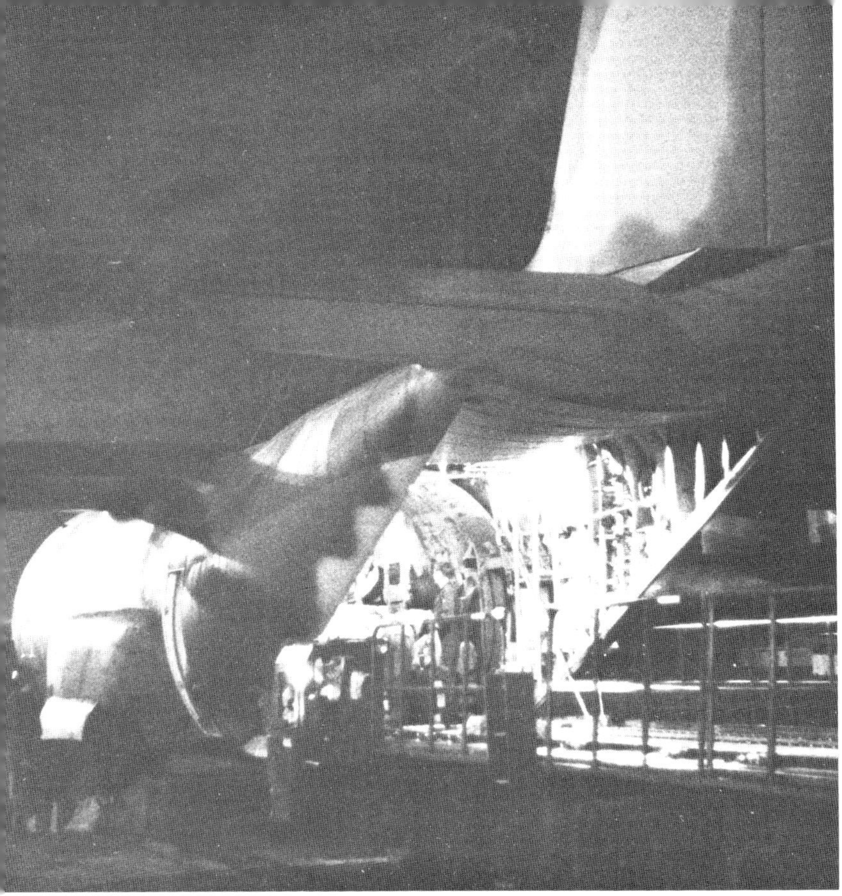

Left and below: 'Old 16 Charlie' on the MAC ramp at Ramstein AB, West Germany during the unloading operations of the turnround before the departure for Mildenhall.

along a purple-fringed funnel towards the runway. From the opposite side of the threshold a C-141 on the south taxiway glared directly at us with its searchlight spread of landing lights nullifying our night vision. Somebody out there got the message and switched off the Starlifter's daylight-making apparatus as we resumed the pre-take-off checks in a restored ambient darkness.

At 108,000lb gross weight (including 22,000lb fuel and 3,000lb cargo), 15,400lb torque, and with the customary half flaps the Herc was due to start flying at 98kts. We turned on to the receding avenue of lights, ran up the engines, brakes off and started to roll. The runway began to dip below the nose as '1293' responded to some back pressure on the control column and we lifted off at 21.09hrs into a partly cloudy night over western Germany. A left turn out on to a northerly heading with the altimeters winding into the climb . . . 28, 29, (3,000ft) 31, 32 . . . Down below patches of amber lighting marked the small communities nestling in the invisible Eifel. The visibility might be good here but the anticipated Mildenhall weather was nothing famous — 1½ miles in fog with a frontal system due to pass overhead at about 22.00hrs; we looked like having front row seats for its passage. Ten minutes out of Ramstein and we had fairly soared past FL 175, the TAS building up to a comfortable 270kts. As we rode west then north over Belgium at 18,000ft we were skating just above the silver coloured cloud tops. Despite the ever-present roar from the four Allison engines it looked a tranquil vista — cotton wool stretching to the horizon (and announcing the oncoming low pressure system), countless stars, and moonlight from the port quarter. The reverie was broken by the flight engineer heading for the 'front office' coffee machine. Polystyrene cups of steaming black liquid in hand we looked at the view ahead; 'This is the best time of the day', said Ken, 'all quiet and peaceful'. With 1,500hrs on Hercs I supposed he was well used to the background noise? He was; and the C-130 experience was a family one as his brother was also serving in MAC and has 6,000hrs on the type! How had it been on TDY? 'I'll be real sorry when we get through this rotation — it's been a lot of fun, especially now the whole drew is together again!' Pete Discenza it turned out had spent part of the TDY period in Turkey, Dave Boyer had been detached to Athens but now everyone was back for the final series of missions before the re-deployment home on 6 October. 'OK, time to go to work again', said Ken, and 1hr 5min out of Ramstein the descent into the UK was started as we throttled back to 250kts TAS.

Thirteen miles east of the coast at Clacton we were passing FL120; Pete Discenza was getting confirmation of the Mildenhall 'weather' and accordingly requesting a Precision Approach Radar talkdown to a full stop. This was acknowledged as we got closer to home, though for runway 11 rather than the 29, which would have allowed us a straight-in recovery. As we tracked eight miles south of Mildenhall on the 'downwind' leg, the before-landing checks were completed and we were cleared down to 2,300ft. Clearance to 1,300ft came with the right turn on to the base leg some seven miles west of the field, followed shortly by a 'turn right to zero nine zero' instruction from the approach controller as he lined us up. The sequence of 'need not acknowledge' transmissions flowed steadily into our headsets.

'Old 16 Charlie you are six miles, check wheels are down.'

'Turn right, heading one two zero'

'Old 16 Charlie, five miles, begin descent'

'On glide path, left of course, correcting'

The murk through which we were flying at 130kts TAS suddenly started to pulsate with a silvery glow from the as yet unseen threshold strobes. 'Got the field at twelve' announced Dave Wood who had been acting as a supernumary lookout for the pilots; and there ahead was the approach lighting with still 3½-miles to run. We were now able to monitor the accuracy of the controller's glidepath and heading instructions on the talkdown: full flaps were wound out at two miles and wishing the brilliancy of the strobes was a bit less pronounced we arrowed across the threshold for a 22.49hrs recovery. Ken called the footage remaining as we rolled out and ended with a 180° turn on the runway to head back for Hardstand 38. Two glowing wands waving at us in the dark signalled our arrival at the correct location and positioned us on the parking spot.

It had been a 7.6hrs (7hr:36min) flying day, making a total of 15hr 18min flight time for the crew on the round trip. The Hercules had carried 108 passengers and an aggregate 18,000lb cargo on the outbound legs, and 119 and 18,800lb respectively on the return stages to Mildenhall. And the next assignment 'off the wall' for 72-1293? The aircraft went and did it all over again, taking the Wednesday- scheduled *European Eagle* out of Mildenhall early the next morning — that's utilization!

Above: The early days of the 'Strathallan Story', and for the passengers aboard Super Courier G-ARMU an eagle's eye view of the glens.

Below: The business end of the airfield at Auchterarder with the offices, hangars and some of the aircraft of the Strathallan Collection.

All photos courtesy R. E. Richardson Esq, Strathallan Aircraft Collection.

The Strathallan Aircraft Collection

John Hunt

Hendon, Le Bourget, Yeovilton, Lucerne, Strathallan . . . any aviation enthusiast will recognise these names as places of pilgrimage, but one museum has some unique claims to fame — the Strathallan Aircraft Collection at Auchterarder, Perthshire. Nestling between the Ochil and Grampian hills this small airfield has the largest number of airworthy WW2 aircraft outside the United States, in what must be the most beautiful and remote location of any museum in the United Kingdom.

Auchterarder airfield is on the estate of Strathallan Castle and was first used by Cirrus Aviation Ltd, trading under the name of Strathair (Strathallan Air Services) which was formed in 1962 by Sir William Roberts. Initial equipment was one Helio Courier, G-APXH, and a Super Courier, G-ARMU, which were used for charter and sightseeing flights, particularly to golf courses, where their STOL (short take-off and landing) ability was needed. One courier was operated into Portree (Isle of Skye) connecting with BEA services at Renfrew (Glasgow) and Turnhouse (Edinburgh) or British Railways at Gleneagles. Some three years later two Piper PA23 Aztec 250's and a DH104 Dove 5 were delivered for charter work and air taxi flights to Turnhouse, Inverness, Prestwick, and Renfrew airports. Strathair was also licensed to undertake scheduled services which connected with BEA, British Caledonian and Emerald Airways flights flying from Prestwick (via Turnhouse) and Dundee to Inverness. For a short period in 1966 one C-47A Dakota, G-APPO, was operated, mostly on crew training; a second C-47B, G-AOGZ, was delivered in 1967 and used for two years on charter flights, its employment including a short spell on charter to British United Airways before being used on oil rig support work out of Aberdeen for BEA.

However, scheduled air services were suspended in 1968 and by 1971 only one Aztec G-APXN remained for air taxi work. After the tragic death of David Roberts in an accident at Gleneagles Golf Course in June 1971, all operations ceased.

Sir William Roberts had always wanted to start a collection of airworthy aircraft from the WW2 era and was going to base them at Flimwell Farm in Kent, where there was a 700yd strip as runway. But after local residents had complained about the likelihood of aircraft noise it was decided to form the collection at Auchterarder. The process of forming the collection began almost by accident in 1969 when the purchase of a Hurricane, G-AWLW, necessitated the acquisition of two twin seat Spitfires in order to clinch the deal. All three aircraft had flown in the film *Battle of Britain* and were sitting at Shoreham awaiting sale. G-AVAV, a Spitfire IXT, was flown up to Strathallan in December 1971 and the second Spitfire, G-AWGB, was sold to Canada in 1970 as CF-RAF. G-AVAV, which had a Cross of Lorraine badge applied to its starboard side, was sold in the USA; and the Mk XIV which had been purchased for rebuilding has subsequently been sold to Spencer Flack at Elstree.

The abiding philosophy behind the Strathallan Aircraft Collection, which has grown from such tentative beginnings to the point where it is now one of the most famous in the world, has been to preserve the aircraft in a flyable condition. As Sir William himself put it, 'The Strathallan Collection is a "live" museum. The work of restoring aircraft and, once restored, maintaining them is a continual progress. While there are arguments for and against flying rare aeroplanes, they were designed to fly, and are "at home" in their element. My ultimate aim is to restore as many as possible of the collection's aeroplanes to an airworthy state.

'I have recently decided on a major change in policy regarding restoration of the Collection's aeroplanes. If the engineers work on one aeroplane to bring it to a fully airworthy state there is a risk that others could deteriorate in storage, whilst awaiting restoration, so I have decided to consider each aeroplane or major component of an aeroplane as an entity, and bring this to a state where it is an exhibit in its own right. The de Havilland Hornet Moth G-ADMT, for example, is exhibited in a dismantled state, but the structure of the aeroplane, normally covered by fabric or plywood, can be seen.'

In line with this policy such aircraft as the Battle, Blenheim, Lysander Lancaster and Swordfish are given priority rebuilds before others, in the collection — eg. the Scion, Dragon and Puss Moth — which although of great

Right: Strathallan's Lysander III has been painted in the markings of No 309 (Polish) Squadron, and the aircraft is seen here suitably weighted down during engine tests in late-1979 which preceded its successful return to flying condition.

AR
V9441

ROYAL CANADIAN AIR FORCE
AIR TRANSPORT COMMAND
976

Left: Some impression of the daunting prospect which can mark the start of an aircraft restoration programme is provided by this view of the fuselage of the Fairey Battle I acquired by the Strathallan Collection in November 1972.

Below: Restoration of the Battle is proceeding under a priority rebuild — the photo shows Dick Richardson working on the aircraft's tailplane.

interest to aviation enthusiasts are not so well known to the public at large. Nonetheless the fuselages of these machines to be restored at a later date, are on show in the new hangar rather than being stored away in order to underline the amount of work required to transform them from their 'before' to their 'after' condition as pristine flying examples of the type.

The Collection's aircraft, although airworthy, are flown very sparingly, mainly at the annual air show and for test flights. There are two main reasons for this — cost and secondly, the need to prolong engine and airframe hours, an objective common to any collection. An example of the desirability of cost restraint was a 'sortie' by the Collection's Mosquito B35 (which had been used in the film *633 Squadron* at Bovingdon and later sold to the Collection by Gp Capt Hamish Mahaddie), when the late Neil Williams flew it from Strathallan to Banff for the re-opening of the flying club field. On the return flight, it had to divert to Prestwick Airport where it was hangered at a cost of £70 a week. Strathallan had to wait four weeks before Neil could return

Left: The Collection's ex-RCAF Lancaster should soon be ready to take to the air again, though in a very different scheme to this post-war modified 'Lanc' which was operated by the service's Air Transport Command.

Below: The Strathallan Mosquito B35, painted as RS712, makes a low pass across the airfield during one of its rare outings.

Below right: An aerial view of the airfield at Auchterarder showing the present 3,300ft long runway and the Comet and Shackleton outside the large hangar. The new runway will align to the left of the present one as seen in this view — from close to the current threshold at the nearer end towards the mound at the top left of the airfield.

and ferry the Mosquito back to Auchterarder, and the total cost of this operation including extra fuel, landing fees and hangarage was £700! Hence the fact that although, many requests are received to fly the Collection's aircraft at air displays the museum has had to decline. The Hurricane, for instance, has only flown 15 hrs since being rebuilt in June 1973.

The Collection's manager Mr R. E. ('Dick') Richardson and his staff of four full time engineers are assisted by part time helpers from the membership of the Strathallan Aircraft Society. The problems which arise in restoring veteran (and not so veteran) aircraft are multifarious — the aircraft have usually been long out of production, often there are no manuals, parts lists or jigs to aid the rebuilding, and parts sometimes have to be fabricated on site. Spare parts however, are less of a problem in view of the minimal flying hrs conducted with the aircraft.

The present runway at Strathallan is 3,300ft long, but a 20° re-alignment is planned which will offer the opportunity of setting out a new

Above: How the Lancaster was seen by Dick Richardson when he first encountered it at St Albert, Alberta on 10 April 1974.

4,000 ft surface. This strip will be more level than the present one, which has a distinct 'dip', and it will also be better aligned with the prevailing wind direction. In some instances the 3,300ft runway was rather marginal; and a story is told of the late Neil Williams which underlined the point as well as showing his attention to safety. Neil always felt that the runway was short for the Mosquito, and when he flew it up from West Malling after the hydraulics had been checked, he made several passes over Strathallan to weigh up the situation before landing the aircraft. The landing was safely accomplished, but the Mosquito ended up only 60yd short of the boundary after heavy braking. Work on the runway re-alignment project is being held up as Pictish remains have been found in a mound that will have to be levelled, and archaeologists are excavating the site.

Once the new runway is completed, then the star of the Strathallan Collection — the Lancaster — will be able to fly once again. Much has been written about the Lancaster and its journey from Canada, but little about the enormous amount of preparation involved. Dick Richardson received a letter asking if Sir William was interested in buying a Lancaster which was located at Saint Albert, an airfield about six miles from Edmonton, Alberta. Dick, who used to work on the RAF Battle of Britain Memorial Flight Lancaster, jumped at the chance of the Collection's acquiring only the second flying Lancaster in the world. He arrived at the Canadian airfield on 10 April 1974 to find a forlorn 'Lanc' sitting in deep snow, bird droppings all over it, one propellor off and some damage to the wing tips, not to mention numerous cigarette ends and litter throughout the aircraft!

After finding a replacement propeller and running up the engines, he found that the Lancaster was basically sound — the engines ran sweetly and all the hydraulic systems functioned normally. In three visits totalling about four months, working in an open fronted hangar and often in sub-zero temperatures, Dick and a dedicated band of engineers gradually put everything to rights. This even included finding the original bomb doors at a farm 70 miles away and re-fitting them; they had been cut out in order to install water tanks for the aircraft's pre-retirement forest fire water bombing role. After spending £42,000 in acquiring and re-furbishing the Lancaster, and naming it *Spirit of Caledonia*, the aircraft was flown across the Atlantic by a British Caledonian crew commanded by former Lancaster pilot Capt P. A. Mackenzie, the ferry flight arriving at Strathallan on 11 June 1975 after recording 32 hrs airborne time. The Lancaster is one of a batch of 430 built by Victory Aircraft in Canada and was flown as KB976 by No 405 'Vancouver' Squadron of the Royal Canadian Air Force from Linton-on-Ouse in 1945: it also holds the distinction of flying the last 'operational' sorties by a Lancaster in April 1964. It was hoped to have matt camouflaged the Lancaster during the winter of 1979/80 and to have completed a re-paint in No 405 Squadron colours, as well as fitting and glazing the front and rear turrets.

A similar epic flight was made by the Lockheed Hudson IV owned by the Collection. The Hudson had served with Nos 2 and 13 Squadrons of the Royal Australian Air Force while based at Hughes near Darwin, and its wartime experiences included strikes against Japanese shipping and bases. Post WW2 the aircraft was used by the Sydney Morning Herald on peaceful bombing missions — dropping newspapers to remote communities in the Australian outback, before being converted for aerial survey work. All that was needed in the way of checks before its flight to the United Kingdom was ultrasonic testing of the propellers and an engine overhaul. On 19 April 1973, Lionel Van Prague, a spritely 63-year-old, accompanied by a qualified airframe fitter and a liberal supply of cigarettes, lifted-off from Kingsford Smith Airport, Sydney and 73 flying hours later landed at Strathallan on 10 May after a flight of 12,000 miles. The Hudson has been re-painted in the markings of No 13 Squadron and is awaiting airworthiness certification. While Sir William Roberts is always on the lookout for additional aircraft for the Collection in the course of his business travels around the world, attempts to purchase suitable examples do not always run so smoothly. In recent years, for examples, the Australian Government's ban on the export of veteran aircraft has meant that a Gipsy Moth bought by the Collection, cannot be shipped into the United Kingdom.

The Collection's famous Hurricane IIB was built in 1942 by Canadian Car & Foundry Ltd, and used for advanced training at Macdonald Manitoba. Surviving until 1952 it was bought by a farmer for its scrap value and used as a childrens' plaything. Recovered by Bob Diemert in 1966 from the farm at Portage la Prairie,

Above: This Lockheed Hudson IV was delivered to the RAAF in 1942 and after a chequered post-war career it arrived at Strathallan in 1973. The aircraft has been restored in representative markings from the latter years of WW2 and with its original serial number, A16-199.

Below: The Hurricane IIB being started up for a test of its Rolls-Royce Merlin engine. This aircraft was one of the 'stars' of the film *Battle of Britain* and a founder member of the Collection built up by Sir William Roberts.

where the wings were found in a nearby creek, it was restored over the next three years and then shipped across the Atlantic to take part in the film *Battle of Britain*. During the production it was flown back to Canada in a RCAF Hercules to take part in a service celebration, and later returned the same way to finish filming. The Hurricane was moved by road from Shoreham to Strathallan, and after further restoration took to the air for its first test flight on 28 June 1973 in the hands of Hawker Siddeley test pilot Duncan Simpson.

Above: The most testing project undertaken by the Strathallan Aircraft Collection to date has been the restoration of another Canadian-built veteran, the Lysander III. The aircraft was acquired in 1971 and is seen during engine tests in late-1979.

Above right: The wings were fitted after a repaint, and on 14 December 1979 the aircraft made two test flights totalling some 45min.

The latest acquisition for the Collection is a Blackburn-built Swordfish II, W5856, one of the batch of 100 with strengthened lower wings completed between October and December 1941 at Sherburn-in-Elmet. This particular aircraft was operated by the Royal Navy until February 1944 when it was handed over to the RAF for tactical aids trials at Manston, later being crated and sold to the Royal Canadian Air Force in May 1945. Mr J. F. Carter, a farmer at Monroville, Alabama bought the Swordfish in 1953 and trucked it from Ontario to his farm for conversion (unsuccessful) into a cropduster. When discovered by Sir William it was still complete, except that the main spar and aircraft framework had corroded due to humidity. The Swordfish has now been completely stripped down and surveyed, but technical drawings are needed before restoration — about a three-year task, can be started. Luckily the Collection has a spare Pegasus engine, so the problems in eventually keeping it airworthy will be less than they could have been.

The histories of the other aircraft in the Collection are all equally fascinating and in most cases exhibit a tremendous diversity of geographical operation — and rescue for preservation! The Collection's former AT-6D Texan, G-AZJD, for example, was ordered by the RAF, completed in 1943, and shipped to the

Union of South Africa. After WW2 it returned to the United Kingdom and was stored until transferred to the Belgian Air Force in February 1947. In August 1958 it was sold to *Compagnie Air France* for pilot training, becoming F-BTBF and based at Pontoise. Sold into private ownership in 1965 it was flown to Strathallan in June 1971. After taking part in many displays it was sold to a private owner at Biggin Hill.

In December 1971, the Texan was joined by a second Harvard IIB, G-AZBN. This aircraft had been constructed in Canada by the Noorduyn Company, delivered to the RCAF as FT391, and later sent to the United Kingdom in 1944. Sold to the Royal Netherlands Air Force in 1947 it was flown by No 306 Squadron before going into storage in October 1961, but after being allocated the Dutch civil registration PH-HON, it was finally sold to the Collection for £1,700 in May 1971.

One of the most recently completed restoration projects, and one which in view of the type's rarity has been keenly awaited, has been that of the Lysander. This is another Canadian-built veteran, manufactured by the National Steel Corporation in 1942, and it served with the Royal Canadian Air Force as '2355'. Purchased from a farmer in Manitoba, who was an ex-RCAF flying instructor, it was shipped over to Southampton in October 1971. The Lysander has been constantly under restoration since then — a total of 8,000 man hours having been spent on it since its arrival, and by late 1979 the aircraft was flying again. The Collection has completed the Lysander in the colours of No 309 (Polish) Squadron, which used to operate the type from Findoe Gask airfield some five miles from Strathallan.

On a visit to Canada in 1972, Sir William traded in one of the Tiger Moths in his collection, G-ANOS, as part exchange for a Bristol Bolingbroke IV T. The Bolingbroke was built in 1942 and used for gunnery and bomber training, and as a tug for target drogues. In 1943 it was damaged in a crash following a fire in the port engine while at the Bombing and Gunnery School at Dafoe, Saskatchewan. After being repaired it was sold in 1946 with 486 flying hours in its log. The museum is restoring it as a Bristol Blenheim IV. Another item in the Collection at a similar stage of re-building as the Bolingbroke is the Fairey Battle I purchased in the US. By the autumn of 1979 its engine propeller, tail

assembly and much of the fuselage had been overhauled.

The Fairey Firefly AS6 was formerly based at RNAS Abbotsinch, before being shipped to Australia in late-1950. Classed as an instructional airframe after four years flying, it was sold in 1960 for scrap. Bought by the Collection in 1973 it was shipped to London for delivery by road to Strathallan. However, as a 12ft-wide load, it was too wide for the journey, and was shipped to Dundee by coaster, making only the final 12-mile part of the journey to Strathallan by road. The Collection's Avenger arrived in a similar way in May 1976 after shipment via Rotterdam from the Hague, where it had been used for instruction at the Anthony Fokker school.

August 1974 saw the most spectacular arrival at Strathallan of any of the aircraft when the Comet 2R, XK655, was 'delivered'. The Comet had nearly come to the end of its fatigue life, and when it was put up for disposal, Sir William decided it should be flown into Strathallan. After much careful planning, the aircraft — second largest in the Collection — came in on a slow approach only to have its starboard undercarriage collapse on landing. It was subsequently repaired by the RAF, and the interior now houses a display depicting the history of de Havilland aircraft. As a result of the Comet incident, the RAF's offer of an Avro Shackleton T4 to the Collection was accompanied by a stipulation that the aircraft would belong to the Collection once the airfield was in sight! The Shackleton, VP293, landed safely in May 1976, and did not live up to its nickname of *Zebedee* for bouncy landings!

The Collection bought a number of civil aircraft in Australia before the earlier-mentioned ban on veteran aircraft exports. One of the acquisitions is a Puss Moth, VH-UQB (G-ABDW) — and, in fact, the oldest aircraft in the Collection. It flew from Croydon to Darwin in 33 days in 1930 and after a long career with Marshall Airways was bought by the Collection in 1973. The DH84 Dragon I, VH-SNB, was the second Australia-built Dragon and delivered to the Royal Australian Air Force as A34-13. After a private-owner career it was operated by a Christian missionary organisation in Australia, and was acquired by the Collection in 1974.

The most interesting aircraft obtained from Australia though is the Short Scion I. Delivered as G-ACUX (later VH-UUP) and equipped with floats for use on a gold surveying project in New Guinea, the Scion once had an oil tank split with the result that an engine seized and it was taxied for 140 miles up a river! The Scion was re-converted to a landplane, served as an air ambulance and after its C of A expired was stored in a hangar at Bankstown aerodrome near Sydney. Found slightly nearer home was

Above left: The Avro Shackleton T4 touches down safely at the end of its delivery flight in May 1976.

Above: How many of Strathallan's aircraft arrive on site! This was the DH Dragon being offloaded from a container after its journey from Australia.

Below: Another newcomer from Australia, the Short Scion acquired in January 1974.

the DH89A Dragon Rapide (Dominie I), now restored in Railway Air Services colours as *Star of Scotia*, this aircraft was flown back from Sri Lanka in 1973, where it had been registered 4R-AAI to Rapid Air.

Finally, a mention of two unique aircraft which have their home at Strathallan, the GAL 42 Cygnet II and the Reid and Sigrist Desford. The Cygnet was the first British all metal tricycle undercarriage aircraft — of only 11 examples built, 'Bravo November' is the last survivor. Built in 1941 it was impressed into the RAF and used on communications duties, being flown by

VZ

Below: The Reid and Sigrist Desford is the sole example of the type: built as a twin engine trainer, it was not adopted by the RAF and later modified for prone pilot trials.

Right: The only surviving example of the Miles M18 basic trainer dating from 1939, G-AHKY.

Sqn Ldr Guy Gibson for a short time during the war, after which it was based at Biggin Hill and used by many private owners. The Desford, G-AGOS, is the sole example ever built and the most unusual aircraft in the Collection. Initially designed as two-seat trainer in 1945, it was sold to the Air Council in 1949 and modified to allow it to be flown in a prone position, being first flown in the configuration in 1951. After five years of trials it was sold to Film Aviation Services for aerial survey and photographic work, and was purchased by the Collection in December 1973 along with six Ansons from Kemps Aerial Surveys in January the same year.

And so to the future: now that the Collection is housed in a weatherproof hangar, work can proceed in the knowledge that the aircraft awaiting restoration are not deteriorating while the preservation activity is centred on prior tasks. Also on show in the hangar is a constantly growing collection of aviation memorabilia. Flying displays are held during the second weekend of July each year and the Museum is open every day from 10.00 — 17.00hrs. The Collection's location is about 1 mile from the B8062 road to Crieff and an hours' drive from Edinburgh or Glasgow.

Acknowledgement
The author would like to extend grateful thanks to Mr R. E. Richardson for his generous assistance received during the preparation of this article. Anyone interested in joining the Strathallan Aircraft Society should write to Mr Richardson at; The Strathallan Aircraft Collection, Strathallan Airfield, Auchterarder, Perthshire.

Aircraft operated by Strathair

Registration	*C/N*	*Type*	*Subsequent History*
G-APXH	061	Helio H391 Courier	w/o Athens 8.11.64
G-ARMU	523	Helio H395 Super Courier	Sold June 1966
G-APXN	27-119	PA27 Aztec 250A	w/o Gleneagles Golf Course 24.6.71
G-ARYG	27-2093	PA27 Aztec 250B	w/o Inverness 22.1.66
G-ATLC	27-3058	PA27 Aztec 250C	Sold 1971. Operated on behalf of Scottish Malt Distillers
G-AVNK	27-3335	PA27 Aztec 250C	Sold August 1970
G-ATWG	30-1094	PA30 Twin Comanche B	Sold November 1968. Operated on behalf of West Highland Woodlands
G-ASDD	04452	DH104 Dove 5	Sold July 1970
G-AOGZ	33282	C-47B Dakota	Sold March 1969
G-APPO	20453	C-47A Dakota	Sold October 1966

w/o = written off

Strathallan Aircraft Collection, Past and Present

Details to November 1979   * Not on public view   † Airworthy

Serial Registration	*Type*	*Date of Acquisition*	*Notes*
G-AGWE	Avro 652A Anson 19/2	Jan 1973	Ex-TX201. For sale — standing at end of runway.
G-AHIC	Avro 652A Anson 19/2	Jan 1973	Sold 1979 to Gordon Fraser
G-AHKX	Avro 652A Anson 19/2	Jan 1973	Stripped down in Museum
G-APHV	Avro 652A Anson 19/2	Jan 1973	Ex- VM 360 Sold to Royal Scottish Museum at East Fortune
G-AWRS	Avro 652A Anson 19/2	Jan 1973	Ex-TX213. Sold to Northumbrian Aircraft Collection
G-AYWA	Avro 652A Anson 19/2	Jan 1973	* Stored in barn on estate.
G-ATBM	Grumman TBM-3W2 Avenger	May 1976	Ex-85650 USN and 045 R Neths Navy
R3950	Fairey Battle I	Nov 1972	
9940 (RCAF)	Bristol Bolingbroke IVT	Dec 1972	
G-AMXA/ XK655	DH106 Comet 2R (Ex-2C)	Aug 1974	First Comet 2, built as G-AMXA in 1953 for BOAC. Used for 4 years in radar installation tests, modified for signal duties with Nos 192 & 851 Sqns RAF.Aircraft did not receive cabin strengthening modifications, so always flew unpressurised with square windows.
G-AGBN/ ES915	GAL 42 Cygnet II	Jun 1975	† Painted as G-AGBN
G-AGOS/ VZ728	Reid & Sigrist Desford	Dec 1973	† Painted as VZ728
G-ALXT	DH89A Dragon Rapide	Aug 1975	Painted in Railway Air Services colours
VH-SNB	DH84 Dragon I	Apr 1974	
WD833	Fairey Firefly AS6	Dec 1974	*
G-AZBN	North American Havard IIB	Jun 1971	† Painted as FT391
G-AZJD	AT-6D Texan	Jun 1971	Sold August 1976
G-ADMT	DH87B Hornet Moth	Dec 1971	Built 1936
G-BEOX	Lockheed Hudson IV	May 1973	Ex-VH-AGJ. Painted as A16-119 RAAF
G-AWLW	Hawker Hurricane IIB	Apr 1970	† Ex-RCAF 5588
G-BEPV	Fokker S11 Instructor	Jan 1977	† Ex-PH-ANK
G-BCOH	Avro Lancaster X	Jun 1974	Ex-KB976

G-AIYS	DH85 Leopard Moth	Apr 1977	† Ex-SU-ABM & YI-ABI. Restored by Mr T. Gardiner. Oldest Airworthy aircraft in Collection.
G-AZWT	Westland Lysander III	Oct 1971	† Ex-RCAF2355
G-AHUJ	Miles M14 Magister	Jan 1974	† Painted as R1914. Built by Phillips & Powis at Reading in 1939. Sold to owner in Perth and languished in garage at Aberdeen before being bought by the Collection.
G-AJOC	Miles M38 Messenger 2A	Nov 1973	* Built Newtonwards 1947. Grounded after glued joints legislation and bought by Collection from farmer at Stonehaven. Now in process of a lengthy restoration
G-AHKY	Miles M18 Mk2	Dec 1975	Ex-U0224 & HM545. Only M18 in existence
G-AFLW	Miles M17 Monarch	Jun 1976	† Used by Rolls-Royce at Hucknall for 20 years
G-ASKB	DH98 Mosquito B35	Feb 1972	† Painted as RS712. Built 1946 by Airspeed at Christchurch. Modified as high speed target tug after service with 2nd TAF in Germany
G-AFPN	DH94 Moth Minor	May 1975	† Built 1939 at Hatfield. Impressed by the Air Council in 1940 as X9297. Used by No 7 Air Gunners School, Stormy Down and No 1 Air Armament School, Manby. Used by succession of private owners until bought by the Collection
G-AFOZ	DH94 Moth Minor	Feb 1973	Destroyed in accident Turnhouse Airport 1975
G-AULU/ VS356	Percival Prentice TII	Sept 1975	Painted as VS356
G-ABDW	DH80A Puss Moth	Aug 1973	Ex-VH-UQB
G-ACUX	Short Scion I	Jan 1974	Ex-VH-UUP
VP 293	Avro 696 Shackleton T4	May 1976	
G-ADPS	BA Swallow 2	Oct 1976	† Built 1935. Stored during WW2, subsequently based Lympne where it made 1½hr pilotless flight
W5856	Fairey Swordfish II	Jun 1977	
WA576	Bristol Sycamore II	Aug 1973	
G-ANFV/ DF155	DH82A Tiger Moth	Apr 1970	† Painted as DF155. Built 1942 by Morris Motors, Cowley. Wartime career with RAF at No 28 Elementary Flying School. Sold to Orkney Flying Club 1953
G-ANTS/ N6532	DH82A Tiger Moth	Apr 1970	* Stored
G-ANOS	DH82A Tiger Moth		Sold in Canada in exchange for Bolingbroke
G-AOEL	DH82A Tiger Moth	Dec 1975	* Stored. Up for sale
G-APGL/ NM140	DH82A Tiger Moth	Apr 1970	* Stored
XD403	DH Vampire TII	Apr 1973	* Being restored by local Aeronautical Society
G-BDYG/ WV493	Hunting Percival Provost TII	Jun 1976	† Painted as 7696M. Ex-6FTS Turnhill & Engineering Unit at Halton. Flew to Strathallan June 1976
PV202	Supermarine Spitfire IXT	Apr 1970	Sold as uncompleted airframe to N. Grace
ML407	Supermarine Spitfire IXT	Apr 1970	Served with No 485 Squadron. Sold to N. Grace
MJ772/ G-AVAV	Supermarine Spitfire IXT	Apr 1970	Sold in USA as N8R May 1975. Ex-Irish Air Corps '159'
G-AWGB	Supermarine Spitfire IXT	Apr 1970	Sold in Canada as CF-RAF July 1970. Ex-Irish Air Corps '163'
NH904	Supermarine Spitfire FR XIV	Sep 1971	Bought from Gp Capt H. Mahaddie. Sold to Spencer Flack, Elstree

Naval Clippers

Paul Beaver

Most of us think of the front-line squadrons when we think of the Fleet Air Arm in Britain; however, there are a number of second-line units without which the Royal Navy would be hard put to manage.

Down at Lee-on-Solent in Hampshire, *HMS Daedalus* is host to No 781 Naval Air Squadron — the 'Naval Clippers'. Formed in 1936, the Squadron has given valuable service ever since, from its time in East Africa as a Fleet Requirements Unit until its varied role of today. Hence its squadron motto is 'Reliability'. One has a tendency to think of the Squadron's role as that of a communications squadron only, but in recent years it has had other tasks, including Admiralty refresher courses and aircrew training. A singular honour was accorded the Squadron in 1953, when it led the Coronation Fleet Review flypast of naval aircraft at Spithead.

During its present commission, FONAC (Flag Officer Naval Air Command) has tasked No 781 Squadron with the following missions:

(1) VIP and general communications, long and short-haul.
(2) Support operations in aid of military exercises and other Defence units in the field.

Above: A Sea Heron C1 of No 781 Squadron on the apron alongside the control tower at RNAS Yeovilton, one of the main points of call on the Clipper Routes. *Martin Horseman*

Right: Sea Devon C20s of No 781 Squadron forming up for the air show flypast described in the accompanying article. *Paul Beaver*

(3) 'Clipper' Flights in the UK.
(4) Search and Rescue (SAR) — the unit's area of responsibility stretching from Beachy Head in Sussex to Start Point in Devon.
(5) Fisheries' protection (from Lowestoft to the Mull of Kintyre).
(6) Dover Straits' shipping patrol.
(7) Light twin-engined aircraft pilot conversion.
(8) To be on call within four hours notice for civil or military emergencies.

To help the Squadron perform these tasks, Sea Devon C20 aircraft were commissioned in 1955, and about half a dozen of these twin-engined aircraft are flown at the time of writing. As the

ROYAL NAVY
XJ324

ROYAL NAVY
ROYAL NAVY

Sea Devons are only five-seater machines, they were supplemented on the long-haul routes, where a greater seating capacity is required, by their larger sister, the Sea Heron, and four remain in No 781's hands. These particular aircraft were once flown by Jersey Airlines. Two Westland Wessex helicopters are on strength, these being VIP adaptations known in the Service as 'Green Parrots' because of their predominantly green colour scheme — the colour of an Admiral's barge. As their name suggests they provide a VIP helicopter service wherever and whenever a Flag Officer needs to visit a place inaccessible to fixed wing aircraft. An obvious example is the inspection of warships by dignatories unable or unwilling to use surface transport.

Left: Sea Devons of No 781 Squadron over the Solent on 21 July 1979, with the Isle of Wight forming the backdrop to the scene. *Paul Beaver*

Top: The two VIP Wessex 'Green Parrots' at their dispersal at Lee-on-Solent; nearer the camera is XT487. *Paul Beaver*

Above: A pair of No 781 Squadron's Sea Herons holding short of the runway at Northolt before a departure for Yeovilton. *Martin Horseman*

The fixed wing aircraft carry the full civil and military navaids to enable them to operate in and out of any civil or military airfield in the British Isles, and the Continent as well. In the UK there are two Clipper Routes which are regularly flown:

(a) Lee-on-Solent — Yeovilton — Prestwick — Glasgow — Edinburgh — Leuchars — Lossiemouth, and back.
(b) Lee-on-Solent — Yeovilton — Exeter — Culdrose, and back.

Above: A major landmark on the route between Northolt and Yeovilton, the power station at Didcot, Berks seen from the southwest during a return flight to London. *Martin Horseman*

The stops at Glasgow, Edinburgh (Turnhouse), RAF Leuchars and Exeter are by request only and although staging points can be incorporated as required, the main Clipper Routes are flown the most regularly.

The SAR facilities in the Solent area are provided mainly by the three Wessex helicopters from *Daedalus'* own Rescue Flight, but fixed wing aircraft can be called in to assist, having the advantage of greater speed to a search area. Also in this mercy category is the Squadron's four hour availability to respond to civil and military emergencies, with the aircraft capable of tasking as personnel and light freight transports.

The British Isles has a declared 200 nautical miles zone of predominantly British fishing and the task of patrolling this vast sea area is now one of the Royal Navy's most important peacetime missions. In order to have the most flexible approach possible and to eliminate many of the operational problems of regular warship patrols by the 'Grey Funnel Line', the Fleet Air Arm has been in the forefront of protection duties since the early 1970s. Not only are helicopters flown from warships flights involved in the so-called 'Offshore Tapestry' patrols used to keep an ever-ready vigil of both deep water and coastal zones, but for the last eight years or so, a fixed wing aircraft has been helping to report, aid and deter foreign fishing vessels — even the occasional British boat sometimes bends the rules. The aircraft used is the veteran Sea Devon light-twin, more commonly seen on communications duties with No 781 Squadron.

In the mid-1970s, the Royal Air Force was becoming more and more involved with offshore patrols, especially in connection with oil-rig security, so the Sea Devon was given a definite, rather than general, patrol zone from the coast to the internationally agreed meridian line. This meant No 781 NAS was to confine its patrols from the Lowestoft area in the east, southwards around the Channel (taking in the Channel Isles) to the Mull of Kintyre. Obviously, it is impossible to patrol this large

Left: The front office accommodation aboard one of No 781's Sea Herons *Martin Horseman*

area with a single aircraft during one sortie, so the task has been rationalised.

Three separate policing areas have been allocated to cover the eastern zone, the southwest and the Irish Sea. The frequency of over-flights depends largely on the weather and the fishing season but, generally, the bulk of the flying hours allowed are given over to patrolling the higher risk western areas. With a little over 15 hours per week flying time, however, the Sea Devon is hard pushed to maintain surveillance.

Despite this problem of low time in the air, the now rather elderly Sea Devon, being economical to run, is an ideal aircraft for flying low-level reporting sorties. The Decca Navigator gear onboard assures that any illegally fishing vessel can be accurately fixed and reported to allow a surface vessel — possibly an 'Island' Class patrol vessel or a Wasp helicopter-equipped frigate — to arrive on the scene to enforce the law, inspect the craft and possibly even make an arrest. As the law currently stands an aircraft cannot arrest a vessel on the high seas; photographic and navigational data, however, can be used as evidence in a court of law.

No 781 Squadron has definite and specific tasks in the fisheries' protection role.

(1) Enforcing the Martime law in liaison with surface vessels by accurately plotting law breakers.
(2) Assisting the Ministry of Agriculture, Fisheries and Food, and Captain Fisheries' Protection, plot the whereabouts of fishing vessels. All sightings are fed into a computer to assist the tasking of protection vessels. In 1978, no less than 1,336 foreign trawlers were sighted and reported by the Sea Devon.
(3) By its mere presence, to act as a deterrent to the fish poacher.

The Sea Devon aircraft employed on this task is quite unmistakable because the aircraft wears a disinctive yellow and blue chequered pennant. This international symbol of fisheries' protection dates back to the last century, although the actual role has been carried out by the Royal Navy for over two hundred years. So next time you visit a coastal airport, from Norwich to Prestwick, look out for the fisheries' protection Sea Devon and give him a wave because, as the Fleet Air Arm's own journal *Flight Deck* put it, '. . . he is protecting your fish fingers . . .'

A very similar sea surveillance patrol is also carried out by Sea Devons of No 781 NAS. In co-operation with HM Coastguards, a Dover Straits' shipping patrol is regularly flown from RAF Manston to identify proven and potential 'rogues' — merchant ships seen by Coastguard radar at Dover to be breaking the 'rules of the road' through this, the world's busiest shipping area. The vessels are identified visually, photographed, and if British registered, are open to legal action when they arrive at a UK port.

The light twin-engined pilot conversion course (SMAC4) was designed to provide aircrew for the Squadron and also for the pilots undergoing training before postings to the Jetstream equipped No 750 Squadron at Culdrose. Since the 1979 re-equipment of No 750's observer training Sea Princes by the

Above: Sea Devon C20, XJ319, wears the Fisheries Protection pennant and 781 NAS badge on its fin. *Paul Beaver*

Right: This Sea Devon C20, XJ350, has black and white striped propeller blades. *Paul Beaver*

Below right: The aircraft in which the author flew during Lee-on-Solent's Air Day, Sea Devon C20 XJ347. *Paul Beaver*

Jetstream it has been mooted that a similar replacement may be on the cards for No 781 NAS; in the interests of standardisation, a communications variant of the navigational trainer at present in service would seem an ideal solution to a replacement problem which has dogged the Fleet Air Arm for the last few years.

The many thousands of visitors who go every year to *HMS Daedalus* at Lee-on-Solent will have seen the 781 NAS massed flypast at the Air Day, with both fixed and rotary wing elements taking part. I was invited to fly with the Squadron during a typical Air Day flypast, a

few years ago. The formation comprised three Sea Herons and four Sea Devons, the author being in the back seat of XJ347. Sitting at the end of runway 28, facing the Solent, Sea Devon '347' was preceded by a Sea Heron and another Sea Devon — XJ319 with the yellow and blue fisheries' protection pennant. While the RAF's 'Bulldog Pair' concluded their precision display, the final checks were completed. '347' was situated in the centre of the formation as the seven aircraft roared off down the runway and this slot was to prove very useful for air-to-air photography during the flight.

Turning to port after take-off the flight flew off towards the Spithead Forts and on this leg the aircraft formed up into the display formation. We continued out towards the Nab Tower and then turned round towards Bembridge from whose airfield a cheeky Cessna 172 flew up to take a look. The flight kept its formation as we travelled on towards and over Ryde and Cowes, being careful to avoid the Air Day holding zone where the Westland Lynx HAS2 from No 702 NAS at Yeovilton was orbiting at low-level before being called in to complete its display. After some 25 min of circling and loose but accurate station keeping, we went in over the Isle of Wight and on a

Above: Sea Heron C1, XR443, and Sea Devon C20, XJ348, as seen from XJ347 during the Air Day sortie; the airfield at Lee-on-Solent can just be discerned at the top of the picture.
Paul Beaver

heading for runway 05 towards the waiting Air Day crowd. On finals the formation tightened up and the helicopters joined us, as together we roared over the crowded lines.

The seven communications aircraft flew in at 1,000 feet turning away towards Fareham, and suddenly the flight broke formation and began landing back at Lee. The airspace was thus cleared for the Wessex 'Junglies' of No 707 NAS to take-off from the northeast side of the airfield to begin the 'rescue' of an 'Arab Sheik' from the last Sea Devon to land back on, in a typical Naval Air Day tableau. So ended a most interesting flight, but for the Squadron, of course, it was only a respite before returning to the normal routine of the weekly Clipper flights.

Acknowledgements
The author wishes to thank Lt M. H. Larcombe RN and No 781 NAS for their kind assistance during many Air Days at *HMS Daedalus*. Thanks are also extended to the Editor of 'Flight Deck' Magazine.

'Learning the Ropes'

W. B. Morrison

Right: A Horsa glider casting its tow rope from an Albemarle tug prior to landing. Albemarles were employed in this role at RAF Brize Norton and this photo was probably taken somewhere over Oxfordshire.

Below: After-dark view of an Airspeed AS51 Horsa I, HS103, being inspected before a night flying sortie. The $3\frac{1}{2}$-ton Horsas were almost equal in size to some of their tugs: fully laden, the gliders grossed nearly 7 tons, and their dimensions are well conveyed in relation to the groundcrew in this picture.
All photos Imperial War Museum, unless otherwise credited

31

Suddenly, the Halifax bomber towing the huge Horsa glider disappeared from sight into a bank of swirling sea fog which engulfed both glider and tug like a wet blanket. With a towing speed of around 150 mph split seconds could mean all the difference between survival or disaster. We had been forced dangerously low over the sea as we headed out from Portreath in Cornwall towards the Bay of Biscay en-route to Sale in North Africa. Sale was in fact in French Morocco, and rather appropriately, one of the other crews engaged in ferrying Horsas to North Africa had taken the lines from a well known song at the time and chalked on their glider 'Like Webster's Dictionary we're Moroccan bound'!

The flights to North Africa were the conclusion of many months of hard intensive training as an Army glider pilot: I had already completed one successful flight, and along with other pilots had returned for a second glider. The date was 7 July 1943. We had been forced back the day before owing to bad weather conditions, and returned to base after being in the air for 2hr 45min.

All the glider pilots were volunteers from various regiments in the British Army and had been selected — until the scheme was cancelled, for training as aircrew in the Royal Air Force. Each volunteer had undergone a very stiff medical test after successfully passing a written examination and going before an Aircrew Selection Board. Naturally, when the scheme to train Army personnel as RAF aircrew was abandoned there was a pool of suitable but 'unused' people available for pilot training and those who had been selected were invited to volunteer to be trained as Army glider pilots for the newly formed First Airborne Division. The idea of using gliders as transports had been approved at high level following their successful use by the Germans in airborne operations, and it was felt that the British forces should also be equipped with glider squadrons.

At the time I was a junior NCO in a Highland regiment and had almost given up hope of ever being able to fly. So when I was asked to volunteer I jumped at the chance, and within a very short while found myself en-route for Fargo Camp, near Tilshead in Wiltshire, where along with other venturesome souls — I was handed over to the tender mercies of instructors from the Brigade of Guards. Those who thought their 'sqaure bashing' days were over were in for a rude and nasty shock — but with few exceptions they put up with it knowing that the so-called failures faced being RTU'ed (Returned to Unit).

Our ultimate role was still rather vague — to us, at least, at the outset of the course, and our peace of mind was rather disturbed when one individual tried to convince us that we were going to fly some form of warhead in *Kamikaze* type suicide missions; but common sence prevailed in the end, and he soon lost his audience. To a certain extent, nevertheless, it was a step into the unknown for British forces in view of the limited Allied experience in the use of gliders for 'Airborne Warfare'.

Civil gliding of course, was, another matter, but there is a world of difference in trying for an endurance or height record in a sailplane, and flying a fully loaded Horsa weighing nearly seven tons into action against ground opposition. In fact flying any type of glider in airborne operations was hazardous, as I was later to experience during the air landing in Greece. Extracting myself from one crashed Waco glider, but having successfully avoided the minefield which had prompted some last-minute, vigorous manoeuvres, I reflected that 'Friday the 13th' was not the best date to be going into action — still, that's another story.

While we awaited our respective postings to various flying schools we were kept occupied in fitness training and also attended a series of lectures given by the commanding officer, Lt Col George Chatterton, a man of outstanding ability and personality who had taken over command following the tragic death in a flying accident of the former CO, Colonel Rock. It fell to Colonel Chatterton to become the driving force which welded a mixed bag of Glider Pilot Regiment volunteers into a fighting force, for not only did the glider pilots fly men and equipment into action but once down, they reverted to their role as soldiers and fought alongside units of the air landing brigade they had helped to fly in. They had to be capable, moreover, of taking over command of a situation if the need arose, whether it meant engaging enemy tanks with 6-pounder anti-tank guns, for example, or leading an infantry assault to secure a vital position.

After the six weeks refresher course at Fargo Camp I was one of those posted to No 16 EFTS (Elementary Flying Training School) at Burnaston Airport just outside Derby where I was to be attached to 'D' Flight. Burnaston was a former private flying field which like several others had been taken over by the RAF to train Army pilots to 'Wings' standard. The training

aircraft consisted of Tiger Moth biplanes and low-winged Miles Magister monoplanes. Some feelings were expressed at first that disciplined soldiers would be difficult to train, it being thought that they would not be relaxed enough to make good pilots, but surprisingly enough we settled down quite happily, and worked hard in both the classroom and in the air to win the coveted wings.

Above: C Flight, No 1 Heavy Glider Conversion Unit, Brize Norton, with the Author in the middle row, extreme right. *Photo via the Author*

Time of course was vital, and the maximum dual instruction allowed before going solo was ten hours, which was considerably less than that taken by some subsequently famous RAF pilots. But no concessions were made on our account — there just was not the time. I had my first initiation flight on 26 June 1942, and after approximately two weeks went solo with 10hr 15min in my log book. It was a fairly stressful period as not only had we to master the techniques of flying but also pass a high standard in navigation and other aeronautical subjects.

There was never a dull moment, and hardly a day went past without something forming the subject for an extended late-evening discussion in the billets after flying and swotting were over for the day. We also had our share of tragedies when someone, or worse if it was a friend from the same flight, 'bought it'. The accidents were not forgotten easily, and still I recall vividly the night a friend and his instructor died in a night flying accident. The wonder is that more of us were not killed or injured, and much of the credit was due to the patience and skill of the instructors who went through some pretty hairy moments before their respective fledglings safely left the nest.

One rather traumatic incident from my own experience happened when I was briefed to take up my Magister trainer and carry out controlled spins. I climbed to the required safety height of 5,000ft and put the aircraft into a spin, but despite going through the correct procedures to pull her out she continued spinning completely out of control. I was on the point of baling out when I realised we were heading towards a town so I remained at the controls to try and steer clear, and luckily managed to regain control with only seconds to spare. What was almost my last flight was a good illustration of the way things could go wrong, and why some of our number never survived to fly in action.

Another experience I could well have done without occurred on my first solo cross country flight. I was on the final leg of the triangular course, and almost back at base, when I ran into trouble. Dense fog suddenly descended upon me. It was like flying into cotton wool, only cold and damp in the open cockpit with moisture clinging to my goggles. In a desperate attempt to get my bearings I took the plane down to 300ft, but the ground and every landmark was completely blanked out. I was lost and alone. Trainers of the type I was flying were not equipped with radio so there was no way I could contact base and advise them of my plight. Another hazard was the very real possibility of flying into the balloon barrage protecting a nearby industrial town whose sprawling factories were a tempting target for low flying enemy radiers. Other aircraft were a hazard too, and the significance of the date, 13 August, did not do much for my confidence!

When I had taken-off on that bright August summer day, the weather was clear and local conditions for the flight were good. I circled the airfield in Tiger Moth DE565, and setting my course on the first leg to Cottesmore, climbed steadily to a ceiling of 2,000ft. The first part of the flight was fairly simple. I had marked out a triangular course on the map, and had to make a turn at Cottesmore before heading onto the second leg toward Anstey where I was obliged to land as it was the check point ahead of the final leg back to base. In due course the Rutland town of Cottesmore loomed up under my starboard wing tip. I made my turn and set course for Anstey. The open country was spread out below me like a patchwork quilt, quite irregular in shape, colour or size. There were no identifiable landmarks so I had to stick to the flight plan. I was quite pleased with myself when eventually I spotted Anstey dead ahead. All these small airfields had grass runways which did not show up too well, and one looked for the tell-tale, bright-orange windsock which caught the eye from a good distance away. There was no radio of course, so I could not ask clearance to land, but just kept a sharp lookout for other aircraft in the vicinity, checked the windsock, landed the aircraft according to the direction of the wind, and reported to the check point in the control tower.

There was no indication at this stage of a change in the weather conditions, and I was given clearance to take-off for the last stage of my flight. I had made good time and was more or less bang on schedule. I got someone to swing the 'prop' and taxied into wind. As the Tiger gathered speed I eased the stick back gently, and with hardly a bounce I was airborne once more. So far the flight had gone well and was almost copybook, but my state of near euphoria was about to be shattered. I was only a short flying distance from base when I ran into trouble. One minute I had good visibility, and the next I had flown into freak weather and was completely blind in a bank of thick fog. It was an alarming experience to be completely cut off and alone in such circumstances. The greatest hazard was the real possibility of a mid-air collision with another aircraft or drifting off-course and flying into the balloon barrage protecting Derby. Without radio I could not contact base or pick up warning signals which would have told me I was approaching the balloons.

I tried to remember all the things I'd been taught which might help to extracate me from the situation. I tried going down but, as already mentioned, I still could not see the ground at 300ft. The only course of action was to climb to a safe height and get clear of the fog. I decided once I was clear of the fog bank to fly a reciprocal course, and then by flying back and forth on that course — ie. the track for the final leg, I ought not stray too far; and with a bit of luck the fog would clear enough for me to see the airfield. In fact I must have crossed the airfield several times before I found a gap and spotted the perimeter far below. I put the plane into a dive through the opening in the fog bank, and made a safe landing.

I was well overdue, and only had a few minutes fuel left in the tank. I learnt afterwards that the general weather conditions were so bad that quite a number of pupil pilots were obliged to force land. My effort which almost ended in disaster won me a commendation in my log book for completing the flight in 'exceptionally bad weather conditions'.

Having successfully completed the initial flying course on powered aircraft at No 16 EFTS, my next stage of training took me to No 4 GTS (Gliding Training School) at RAF Kidlington, Oxfordshire, where I joined 'C' Flight and along with my fellow pupil pilots was introduced to the Hotspur Mk II glider. The gliders were designed to carry ten men including the two pilots who sat in tandem. The machines had RAF markings and were painted in the familiar brown and green camouflage. The towing aircraft were Hawker Hectors and Hawker Hinds both of which were powerful biplanes in their era and had been armed with a Vickers gun forward and a Lewis gun aft. The Hind was earlier classified as a light bomber, and could carry a 500lb bomb load.

The Hector's role was army co-operation; it carried a smaller bomb load than the Hind or alternatively could carry supply containers under the wings. Speed at varying operational heights was in excess of 180mph and alongside the gliders on the ground they looked massive compared to the sleek lines of the comparatively tiny Hotspur.

The course marked my first experience of 'gliding', and after being used to powered aircraft the absence of noise in free flight (except for the swish of the wind over the wing surface) was quite exhilarating. One felt completely detached, like a bird on the wing, but our sense of security was soon dispelled. Shortly after my arrival at Kidlington two crews were killed carrying out a tactical dive approach — a maneouvre designed to bring a glider in fast at low level to beat ground defences. Both crews were in my billet and it was a bit shattering to lose 25% of our number in one morning. Because of the high risk involved, student pilots were subsequently banned from carrying out this manoeuvre on their own.

On one occasion I was with an instructor who was an exponent of the dive approach tactic, and he demonstrated the technique to me. We went into the dive off a stall turn and at the crucial moment the instructor heaved back the stick. We sank at an alarming rate as we came out of the dive, sped like a rocket over the perimeter fence with only feet to spare, and touched down scaring everybody in sight.

After completing my basic training on Hotspurs, I returned to an Army depot in Wiltshire where, at a special 'wings' parade we received the coveted glider pilot wings from General 'Boy' Browning who commanded the British First Airborne Division. While passing down the ranks the General enquired of each man how many hours flying he had done (the average was about 150hr) and his previous unit before joining the Regiment. After congratulating the recipient he hooked small replica wings into a pin above the left breast pocket, and proceded down the lines until all had been given their wings.

In due course I was transferred to 'C' Flight No 1 HGCU (Heavy Glider Conversion Unit) at Brize Norton, Oxfordshire, to complete my training. The adjustment from flying trainers to handling huge 3½-ton gliders was considable. The Horsa gliders were almost equal in size to the towing aircraft, which on training exercises were Armstrong Whitworth Whitleys and

Below: General Aircraft GAL48 Hotspur II, BT615, on tow; the Author completed his basic training on this type.

Armstrong Whitworth Albemarles. Both of those tug types were twin-engined bombers converted for towing, and in fact the Airspeed Horsa's wing span of 88ft was 11ft more than that of the Albemarle. The enormous gliders were capable of carrying squads of fully equipped airborne infantary, 6-pounder anti-tank guns and their towing jeeps plus ammunition, etc. A fully laden Horsa weighed just under seven tons and some idea of their size can be gained from the accompanying photographs.

The gliders were crewed by two pilots sitting side by side at dual controls. The co-pilot's role was to act as an observer and assist in the flying of the glider. He also took over the controls in action if the first pilot was hit. To assist in landing the gliders were also fitted with huge flaps like barn doors, which were operated by compressed air at 200lb/in^2. Such was their braking power that with full flap a direct descent could be made from 2,000ft over the runway. The Horsas were also furnished with air brakes on the landing wheels.

Although the Horsa was equipped with a tail trimming facility, and very effectively so as it once saved two of us during a test dive, one disadvantage was the lack of an aileron trim, which imposed considerable strain on the pilots who had to fly the gliders on long flights. The American Waco, or Hadrian as it was called in British service, did have the advantage of all round trim, and was much easier to fly; anyway it was of course a much smaller glider. The Americans had in fact gone a stage further and had fitted a form of automatic pilot device to one of their larger gliders, but regrettably we never had the opportunity to fly one.

Communication between the Horsa and its tug was by two methods, one being the TR9 radio receiver and transmitter and the other a telephone using the tow rope to carry the line. The latter method was essential where radio silence had to be maintained to avoid signals being intercepted by the enemy — as on the operational deployments to North Africa. Things did not always go smoothly, however, and not always because of a fault in the equipment. On one occasion I was flying troops from the Airlanding Brigade on an air experience exercise when we ran into turbulence, with the result that most of them became airsick. I tried to raise the tug captain on the radio using the normal procedure; 'Matchbox calling tug, are you receiving me?' There was no reply despite repeated efforts to get through and request a return to base, with the result that at the end of the flight my passengers

Left: Underside view of a Horsa in free flight; note the flaps in the 'half' position.

Right: The rudimentary interior comforts of a Horsa, the troops sat on the inward facing bench seating.

Below: Horsas being loaded by airborne forces using special ramps for heavy equipment being installed via the side cargo door.

Above: This side view of a Horsa on tow shows an Austin Motor Co built Mk 1, DP726. Note the towing method, a yoke system with anchorage points under both wings.

were in a bad way. The tug pilot admitted afterwards that he had turned down his receiver because of static in his ears!

On another occasion, two of us with an instructor were trying for a height record behind a Whitley tug when the tow rope snaked back as we circled and got caught around the glider's port wing — with the result that the telephone link broke down. We were at 8,000ft and icing up fast. The rope was jammed and could not be released, and without a tail gunner to act as observer the tug captain did not realise we were in trouble. The instructor ordered us to fasten our 'chutes and stand by to bale out. My colleague and I didn't fancy a free fall from that height, but dutifully donned our parachutes and stood by the loading door ready to release it and jump. At the very last minute, however, the tug captain decided he could not get any higher, and realising something was wrong released us from his end. Once free, the strain was off the wing and much to our relief we were given the order to stand down. It was the second time in my flying career that I had prepared to abandon an aircraft.

Having satisfactorily, if somewhat precariously, completed my conversion course on heavy gliders I was posted for a month to RAF Hurn and then to No 6 MU (Maintenance Unit) Brize Norton where a number of us were involved in ferrying newly assembled gliders to operational airfields all over eastern England. It was on one of these flights that my luck nearly ran out for the last time.

We were scheduled to fly two new Horsas to a base in East Anglia, and the pilot asked if I would mind changing gliders as the registration number on his included the figure '13'. Having been born on the 13th I was not too worried about the significance of the number, and agreed on a swap. In the absence of a co-pilot I had a member of the maintenance staff as 'ballast' in the co-pilot's seat. These gliders were not fully operational, and to maintain contact with the tug I had a makeshift radio control panel strapped to my knee. Without a co-pilot all the work devolved upon me, so when there was an unexpected loss of airspeed shortly after take-off at 800ft — the tow rope had become disengaged from the Albemarle tug — I found myself having to make some snap decisions. I could not see a reasonable landing site anywhere and I was losing height all the time. In the end I was forced to pick a small field away from livestock, and on my final approach I found we were heading for a railway embankment flanked by tall trees — a really confined trap.

There was only one thing to do — turn the wheel hard over to starboard to put my wing into the ground. It was a very fortunate decision because as I swerved to starboard my port wing sheared through some high tension cables, the

Above: A Halifax tug labours into its climb-out after take-off with a Horsa on tow: This view provides an alternative angle on the yoke towing system.

large poles breaking like matchsticks and missing the cockpit by inches. We finished up on the railway line, avoiding an express train by only a few minutes. Fortunately neither of us was seriously hurt beyond facial cuts from flying perspex, but the glider was a complete write-off. I was checked out by the MO who packed me off to the billets with instructions to take the sleeping capsule he had given me. However, I sneaked out to the airfield and persuaded a startled glider crew to let me go aloft to test my nerve. I must have looked a bit frightening with my head swathed in bandages but having proved I felt none the worse for my experience, I returned happily to my quarters.

The first thing the CO asked me when I reported to him the next morning was, 'did you go up again?' When I confirmed that I had done so, his only comment was, 'good, if you hadn't I'd have sent you up!' He wasn't being hard, just being practical. Trained pilots were not only expensive but in our case few in number, and a quick flight straight after a crash was important in restoring one's nerve. I eventually returned to RAF Hurn for advanced training and night flying. The latter required skill and concentration for, as was often pointed out, you only get one chance with a glider — muff it, and there are no engines to take you round again. There were the occasional humourous incidents, however, such as the night when a Horsa crew mistook the flying boat flare path in Poole harbour for their own, and ditched alongside the tender which had put out to pick up the crew from what was scheduled to have been a Walrus seaplane!

On one particular day volunteers were called for to undertake special training for a secret mission, and along with some others I found myself en-route to RAF Holmsley South where we were introduced to the huge four-engined Stirlings and Halifaxes which were to be our tugs. Crews were made up of three glider pilots who were taken up for nine-hour endurance flights — we had been selected to fly Horsas to North Africa where a base had been set up at Sale in French Morocco. The gliders were to be flown out to the Mediterranean theatre in preparation for the invasion of Sicily. It was important to stay aloft for the time laid down as once over the sea and past the point of no return there was no going back, so we had to stick it out at all costs as the tug would not have enough fuel to get us safely back to England.

When it came to my turn to take part in an endurance flight with two other pilots (we operated a rotation system with one pilot resting while the other two remained in the cockpit) we ran into some really bad turbulence. As I was resting we hit one particular air pocket and dropped 200ft. Spreadeagled in the air like a weightless astronaut, I hit the deck with a resounding crash as we pulled out. The two pilots in the cockpit became air sick and I was called to take over control. All three of us were pretty groggy but equally determined to keep going. Almost overcome with nausea I was afraid I might pass out at the controls, and as neither of my colleagues could have reacted quickly enough to take over, the consequences would have been disasterous. In desperate situations one's thinking processes seem to sharpen, especially when motivated by self-preservation, and I suddenly remembered a use for the drinking water in our water bottles. The trick worked — I got one of the other pilots to pour some water down the back of my neck to revive me, and managed to fly the glider on my own for four long hours, finishing with a successful landing. My arms were so stiff and full of cramp that it took some time before I could restore movement in them.

Part of our training included visits to Bournemouth baths for ditching drill, where we donned flying suits and Welington boots, and were obliged to jump in at the deep end. We then had to swim to an RAF-type inflatable dingy and scramble on board. We also had to learn how to get a capsized dingy right way up — no mean feat in a wet flying suit with Wellington boots full of water, especially if you had to assist a fellow pilot who was in some difficulty. It was not too bad if you were lucky enough to start with a dry flying suit, but for sheer discomfort there's little to beat pulling on a soggy flying suit and equally saturated Wellington boots. However, there was one minor consolation in that we did not have to jump into the swimming pool off the top diving board like the fighter pilots who were also undergoing the course.

Eventually the day came that our intensive training and preparation was at an end and along with a number of other glider pilots I was posted to Portreath in Cornwall, where we were to await our turn to fly out Horsas to North Africa — when weather conditions permitted.

For some crews the flights were to terminate in a watery grave far out in the Atlantic after they had been intercepted and shot down by Junkers Ju88s or Focke-Wulf Condors operating from bases in France. Some crews were fortunate enough to be picked up from their dingys, though in one particular case it was over a week before they were found. Others, however, simply disappeared without trace before a distress call could be sent out. There was a laid down procedure in the event of air attack and that was for the Horsa pilot to cast off and ditch. This action enabled the Halifax's tail gunner to traverse his guns and fight off the enemy aircraft without the Horsa obstructing his sights, and it also enabled the tug pilot to take evasive action. Meanwhile the Wireless Operator could send out a distress call so that naval units could make for the spot where the Horsa had ditched.

We had a fighter escort for part of the flight consisting of three Beaufighters which rendezvoused with us off the Scillies, but their range could only take them as far as the Bay of Biscay. To reduce weight they flew without an observer and were given the course for home by the tug's navigator who used the Aldis lamp from the astradome to signal them. Once the

escort left it was then open season and we were prey to any German aircraft in the vicinity. Not only did we have to keep a sharp lookout for enemy aircraft, but scan the sea below for any tell-tale orange blob which could be a dinghy with survivors; and we also kept watch for enemy submarines.

I considered myself very fortunate to have completed two operational deployments without being intercepted, and my worst experience, as described, was merely having to fly blind in thick sea fog. But had it not been for two strange twists of fate I would have subsequently taken part in the invasion of Sicily. The first piece of fortune was the result of a mistake back in England when the spare undercarriage for the glider was loaded. When carrying out long operational flights such as the one described, we released the main undercarriage after take-off to reduce wind resistance to help the tug save fuel. The landing was effected on a skid which was permantently fixed under the fuselage. A spare undercart was carried in the glider and fitted after arrival in North Africa to enable the glider to be flown to its operational base. On this occasion we discovered en-route that instead of having separate port and starboard wheels they were both the same, so the glider could not be flown out from Sale. The tug pilot felt that the best course of action was to fly us directly to the forward area as we could well be required to take part in the invasion if replacements were needed. So on we went, but fate took a hand again as the Halifax developed engine trouble. It turned out later that wind-borne sand has been getting into the intakes, and compounding the tug's difficulties there were hydraulic problems with the undercarriage. The upshot was that the Halifax was obliged to make a forced landing on a disused French airstrip — a task which the pilot completed with commendable skill. We were eventually flown out by a rescue aircraft, but were too late to take part in the invasion. In my case it was a fortunate mishap as the other pilot I had arranged to crew with and my replacement were killed in action during the assault on Sicily.

As it turned out my own baptism of fire was not long in coming, but with the benfit of over a year's training and follow-on experience, I and my fellow glider pilots were as ready as we could be for the trials which lay ahead. We had 'learnt the ropes' and, perhaps more importantly, the tasks which would ensue once our tow ropes were released at the outset of a combat mission.

(The author went on to complete a further five year's service in the Glider Pilot Regiment, taking part in operations in Yugoslavia, South France, and Greece; and being mentioned in dispatches for his service in the Mediterranean theatre — *Ed.*)

Below left: The huge wingspan of the Horsa is well illustrated in this photo of No 3 Horsa Squadron taken at Comiso in southern Italy. Also shown are the squadron's two mascots, Italian mountain dogs named Romulus and Remus.
Photo via the Author

Below: Horsas in their combat arena — in this case during the Arnhem landings in September 1944.

Prototype pictorial

a look back at some post WW2 British research aircraft

Peter Gilchrist

Above: The de Havilland DH108 was designed to investigate the behaviour of swept wings and to provide some basic aerodynamic information for the Comet and the DH110 fighter — eventually to enter service as the Sea Vixen. TG283 was the first of three aircraft to be built under Specification E18/45 and it flew for the first time on 15 May 1946. All three aircraft were built entirely of wood and each fuselage was a standard Vampire unit taken directly from the English Electric Co's line at Preston. The prototype was destined for slow-speed work and equipped with generous leading-edge slats and wing-tip mounted anti-spin parachutes. The other aircraft were more streamlined and aimed specifically at transonic research. During their brief lives these three aircraft pushed aerodynamic knowledge to its limits and VW120 — the third machine to fly — became the first British aircraft to exceed the speed of sound. Finally, all three 108s were lost in fatal accidents: TG306 and VW120 breaking up at speed, while TG283 failed to recover from a stalling test. *MoD(PE), RAE Farnborough*

Above: The Saunders Roe SR.A1 made its first flight from Cowes on 14 July 1947 and being the only flying boat jet fighter ever produced in Britain, it has a unique place in aviation history. It was never proposed to put the type into quantity production but three were built under Specification E6/44 to carry out research into the feasibility of using such an aircraft in an air defence role. Runways have always been vulnerable to battle damage and operation from water obviously eliminated this problem, but a bulky flying boat hull reduced turning radius and manoeuvrability to such an extent that the aircraft itself became vulnerable. The concept was finally abandoned during 1950 but the first prototype, TG263, still survives today at Duxford. The second and third aircraft were both lost in accidents: TG267 crashed while on a routine flight near Felixstowe and TG271 — the aircraft shown here — hit a semi-submerged baulk of timber at high speed and sank almost immediately. *Saunders-Roe Ltd*

Below: In its own way the Armstrong Whitworth AW52 was one of the most exciting aircraft in the air during the late-1940s. Two were built to Air Ministry Specification E9/44 and their theoretical advantages held great promise for the future. The idea was to eliminate the drag of a conventional fuselage and tail — a concept that had often attracted aerodynamicists with its potential for increasing range and efficiency. Unfortunately the results from the AW52 were disappointing: despite the use of laminar flow principles to build the wing and advanced boundary layer control systems to suck 'dead' air away from the control surfaces, the aircraft could never reach its anticipated performance index. True laminar flow was never properly maintained and pitch control was always less than positive because the long elevator lever-arm afforded by a conventional layout was impossible to achieve on a tailless aeroplane. During May 1949 one of the aircraft crashed after severe flutter vibration had spread along the entire wing: the second machine was finally broken up in 1954 after several years of research flying at Farnborough. *Armstrong Whitworth Ltd*

Above: The Avro Ashton was a curious mixture of styles and technologies. Based on the Tudor airframe, the aircraft was pressurised, powered by four 5,000lb thrust Nene engines and equipped to the highest standards then available to allow prolonged flying at altitudes of up to 40,000ft. Specifically designed to provide a broad base to an extensive high altitude research programme, six were ordered by the Air Ministry and the first of these flew on 1 September 1950. After the initial flight tests, the first aircraft was delivered to Boscombe Down. During the following two years the remaining five aircraft were progressively completed and despatched to Farnborough, Defford and Martlesham Heath, where they were flown on individual research projects ranging from pressurisation and temperature control to radar bomb-laying and engine testing. After the early period of altitude-related experiments, four of the Ashtons went on to become useful engine test-beds, carrying various powerplants in representative nacelles under the fuselage or outer wing panels. All six aircraft accumulated many hours of accident-free flying before being retired and broken up at intervals between 1959 and 1962.
MoD(PE), RAE Farnborough

Above right: The Avro 707B flew for the first time on 6 September 1950. It was designed under Specification E15/48 to investigate the low-speed handling qualities of the delta wing planform in readiness for the Avro 698 bomber — later to become the Vulcan. The first prototype 707 VX784, had crashed near Farnborough only three weeks after its first flight and the much delayed VX790 incorporated a number of modifications following the investigation of that accident. The single Derwent engine was fed through a large dorsal intake and this caused problems at the upper end of the speed range. The complex airflow immediately aft of the cockpit created a troublesome pressure drop in the engine and despite several modifications to the intake lips the configuration was never completely satisfactory. The three subsequent 707s were fitted with wing-root intakes and VX790 had a relatively brief career before being scrapped at RAE Bedford.
MoD(PE), RAE Farnborough

Right: The Avro 707A was originally designed around a Derwent engine and a large dorsal intake but in view of the problems suffered by the earlier 707B, it was decided to redesign the aircraft to accommodate intakes in the wing-roots. It was felt that this arrangement would give a more stable performance at high speed and be more representative of the Avro 698 bomber. The new configuration was covered by Specification E10/49 and the aircraft, WD280, made its first flight on 14 June 1951. After about a year, powered flying controls were fitted to extend the aircraft's useful life and eventually the wing was modified to represent the cranked leading edge of the Vulcan. A second 707A was ordered in 1952 and this was delivered to Farnborough as WZ736, in readiness for a period of general research into the control and stability characteristics of delta wings. Both aircraft are now preserved: WD280 in Australia (where it spent its final flying years in support of a research programme sponsored by the Department of Supply) and WZ736 as part of the RAF Museum's reserve collection at Cosford. *MoD(PE), RAE Farnborough*

VX790

Top: Air Ministry Specification E27/46 called for a general purpose research aeroplane, fitted with a delta wing and capable of flight at transonic speeds. A submission was accepted from the Boulton Paul Aircraft Co and their machine was flown as the P111 on 6 October 1950. The aircraft was a classic 45° delta and offered yet another solution to the new problem of intake configuration. Boulton Paul had gone for a large, oval opening in the extreme nose and had provided a bifurcated duct to carry the air around the pilot and nosewheel bay. This layout inevitably gave the fuselage a large cross-sectional area and effectively limited the attainable Mach number to around 0.94. Half way through its career, VT935 was extensively changed internally and four large, petal-type airbrakes were flush-fitted around the fuselage, immediately aft of the cockpit. It returned to its research tasks in this new form as the P111A on 2 July 1953. Although the aircraft was never flown supersonically it did complete many years of useful flying for the RAE at Bedford before being retired to the College of Aeronautics at Cranfield in 1959. From there, it was taken by road to Bagington, where it currently resides as part of the Midland Air Museum.
MoD(PE), RAE Bedford

Above and right: Wartime experiments by German aerodynamicists had clearly shown the advantages of swept wings on an aircraft moving at high speed but the low speed behaviour of these new shapes was little understood. When Specification F23/49 — later to emerge as the Lightning — was issued, a sharply swept wing was proposed for the RAF's first supersonic fighter and much work needed to be done to ensure its safety at low speed and during landing. An Experimental Requirement (ER100) asked the industry to consider what might be called a 'slow Lightning', with the same overall geometry as the proposed new fighter, but aimed specifically at speeds below 350kts. Short Bros & Harland Ltd came up with the SB5. This aircraft, WG768, was completely unique because the wings and horizontal tail could be moved around — though not in flight — to create several 'different' aeroplanes and therefore give the best possible chance of securing a successful formula for the new fighter. Sweep angles could be fixed at 50°, 60° or 69° and various leading edges could be attached to the wing without major engineering problems: the horizontal tail could be positioned at the top of the fin or beneath the fuselage and was fully controllable within a 20° arc, in addition to having normal elevator control. The non-retracting undercarriage of the SB5 could swivel to compensate for various sweep angles and adjust against a vertical line to cope with the centre of gravity changes that follow wing sweep. This cleverly designed aeroplane flew very successfully from 1952 until it was finally retired in 1968, after spending its last few operational years with the Empire Test Pilots School at Boscombe Down. The SB5 is now preserved at Cosford.
Short Bros & Harland Ltd; and MoD(PE), RAE Bedford

BALLAST

Above: Throughout its service career the Rolls-Royce TMR (Thrust Measuring Rig) was known as the 'Flying Bedstead' because of its obvious visual appeal. It's certainly hard to believe now, but this crackling monster was a sensation when it first appeared in 1953. Consisting of little more than two Nene engines held together with a steel space-frame, it was Britain's first attempt at jet-borne VTOL flight. The efflux was driven vertically downwards from nozzles immediately beneath the pilot's seat and attitude control was maintained by four 'puffer-jets' built out on long arms. It was never proposed to fit wings on the TMR and any transition to 'normal' flight was obviously out of the question; the machine was strictly a hovering test rig, although it did carry the aircraft serial XJ314. Rolls-Royce used it for their own experiments before handing it over to the RAE at Bedford in January 1957. After an accident at Bedford it was decided not to repair the machine to flight standards but to give it to the Science Museum for exhibition in London.
MoD(PE), RAE Bedford

Right: The tiny Fairey FD1, VX350, seen here over the Farnborough control tower during 1954, was the smallest aircraft flying in Britain at the time. With a wing span of only 19ft 6in — ten feet less than a Tiger Moth! — the aircraft was originally conceived as a vertical take-off interceptor. Rolls-Royce had prepared plans for a 'special' turbojet with sufficient power to lift the FD1 from an inclined ramp; control during the ascent was to be achieved by ducting hot gases through variable nozzles surrounding the jet efflux under the tail. As it turned out, the VTOL idea was abandoned before the aircraft was completed and the airframe was changed to suit the needs of a more orthodox research programme. It spent most of its time at Boscombe Down and Bedford, flying with a number of different tail and control configurations and adding considerable knowledge to a programme that was the main preoccupation of the mid-1950s, that of delta aerodynamics.
MoD(PE), RAE Farnborough

Above: The Fairey FD2 will almost certainly be remembered for its successful attack on the world air speed record during March 1956. It smashed the American domination in this field by no less than 310mph, and pushed the absolute speed record from 822.26mph to 1,132mph. The machine used for the attempt was WG774, the first of two identical aircraft built to Experimental Requirement ER103. Because record success is the stuff of history books, there is a tendency to forget that the FD2s were eminently successful in their own field of high speed aerodynamic research and their accumulated experience of flying at speeds in excess of Mach 1.5 had a profound effect on future aircraft design. Both aircraft are now fully retired from flying. WG774 was converted at Filton into the BAC221 and flew for several years in direct support of the Concorde programme, before being taken to the Museum of Flight at East Fortune for permanent preservation. The second aircraft, WG777, retained its original FD2 identity throughout its research career at RAE Bedford and finally retired to join the growing number of preserved research aircraft at Cosford. *MoD(PE), RAE Bedford; and Peter Gilchrist*

Above: XG905 was the second Short SC1 to fly, but it was the first to complete a full transition from normal wing-supported flight, through a vertical descent to the hover, and then back to normal flight again. It did this at RAE Bedford on 6 April 1960 and gave Britain an impressive lead in VTOL technology. The two SC1s had been designed around the new, lightweight RB108 engine from Rolls-Royce. This engine was conceived following successful flight trials with the Nene-powered TMR (the 'Flying Bedstead') and had a remarkable power-to-weight ratio of 8:1. Each aircraft was supported vertically by four of the new engines, mounted in pairs on common, gimballed axes, so that they could be collectively tilted fore and aft through an arc of 35°: this swinging of the engines was a clever piece of design that assisted acceleration and deceleration during the transition, as well as giving the SC1 considerable freedom in pitch. The normal propulsion engine was another RB108, inclined at 30° under the tail of the aircraft, with a Tristar-style duct to eject the gases horizontally. The first aircraft, XG900, was taken from Sydenham to Boscombe Down during March 1957, to begin a series of checks before its first flight as a conventional aeroplane on 2 April. At this stage, no lift engines were fitted. The second aircraft made its first flight in a tethering-rig at Sydenham during May 1958, starting a long series of hovering trials that would gradually increase the aircraft's freedom of movement until full transition was achieved. After many years of remarkable flying, both aircraft were retired from Ministry service and preserved: XG900 went to the Science Museum reserve collection and XG905 to the Ulster Folk & Transport Museum. *MoD(PE), RAE Bedford*

The Bristol T188 was hailed as a world beater after its first flight in April 1961. It certainly looked the part: built almost entirely of high-strength stainless steel alloys, it was designed to investigate the thermal and aerodynamic problems associated with sustained speeds in the region of Mach 3.0. Experimental Requirement ER134 was issued in 1952 and presented the industry with the most challenging set of problems it had ever received. These problems were to lead to an unnecessarily prolonged development time and result in an aircraft that was too big and too heavy to do an effective job at its design speed. Two aircraft were eventually flown: XF923 — seen here at Filton immediately before its first flight — and XF926. Both aircraft were powered by two 10,000lb thrust (14,000lb with reheat) Bristol Siddeley Gyron Junior DGJ.10Rs, engines that were always over-stretched in trying to push nearly 40,000lb of aeroplane and fuel up to its operational height before a Mach 3 calibration run could even be contemplated. Fuel consumption was so excessive that average flight times were reduced to around 30 minutes and the longest single flight ever acheived was 48 minutes (all of which was below supersonic speed). In restrospect, the one part of ER134 that probably destroyed the effectiveness of the T188 programme was the insistence on conventional take-off and landing. While the Americans were achieving phenomenal performance with air-launched research vehicles, the T188 was using 70% of its available fuel to reach operational height, leaving almost nothing for acceleration, supersonic cruise and safe recovery. Perhaps in-flight refuelling could have saved the project, but in the event this technique was never used and the maximum speed reached before the programme was abandoned in 1964 was Mach 1.8.
Bristol Aircraft Ltd

Below: This fascinating aeroplane is the Hunting H126, built during 1962-3 to Experimental Requirement ER189D. Its primary purpose was to research the 'jet flap' principle as a means of controlling aircraft at very low speeds. Up to 95% of the efflux from a single Orpheus engine could be directed into the wings, to emerge as a thin gaseous sheet over the top surface of the flaps: the stream followed the contour of the flaps and effectively increased area by forming a cascade of high-velocity gas behind the wing. Normal propulsion nozzles were provided (just visible beneath the wing) but these were fitted with thrust spoilers to enable the pilot to control the proportion of thrust being delivered through the wing ducts. For control at very low speeds, the normal aerodynamic surfaces were supplemented by high-velocity gas jets in the wing tips and extreme tail. The H126, XN714, made its first flight on 26 March 1963 and spent most of its working life at RAE Bedford. During 1969 it was loaned to the Ames Flight Research Centre in California, returning nearly a year later to immediate retirement. It was presented to the Cosford Aerospace Museum in 1974. *MoD(PE), RAE Bedford*

Left: The slow speed handling problems associated with slender delta wings began to exercise aerodynamicists as soon as the Anglo-French Supersonic Airliner — later to become Concorde — had been defined. They were particularly concerned about the Dutch-rolling characteristics of this kind of aircraft and the Handley Page HP115 was built to carry out a variety of flight tests on the planform. The aircraft was powered by a single Viper engine, mounted high on the rear fuselage to minimise airflow disturbance over the wing. Because it was essentially a slow speed aeroplane, the undercarriage was kept simple and fixed, and the large control surfaces were fabric covered. The wing was fitted with an easily detachable leading edge, to enable different shapes and sections to be compared in flight. Two smoke generators — just visible in the photograph — were used to trace the vortex pattern over the wing and the results were filmed by a camera mounted in the fin 'bullet'. After its first flight from Bedford on 17 August 1961, XP841 spent its complete working life on the airfield until it was finally retired during 1973. It was flown for the last time on 1 February 1974 when it left Bedford for Colerne, eventually finding its way to Cosford by road in October 1975. *MoD(PE), RAE Bedford*

Below: Under the terms of Experimental Requirement ER193D, the Filton Division of BAC completely re-built the first prototype Fairey FD2, WG774, to conduct research into the properties of the unusual delta wing that would be used on Concorde. The re-structured aircraft flew for the first time on 1 May 1964 and was known as the BAC221. The original fuselage was lengthened by six feet and the engine intakes were re-positioned under the leading-edge of the ogival wing: fuel tankage was increased and the hydraulic and electrical systems were completely re-designed. A new, much taller undercarriage was fitted and an Elliot autostabilisation system was used to simulate certain unstable conditions during the flight tests. The wing was fully pressure-plotted and a cine camera was built into the top of the fin to record wool tufting experiments. The new aircraft retained the original 'drooping' nose of the FD2, but it was made fully controllable rather than simply fixed in the up or down positions. The 221 spent nearly ten years at RAE Bedford, working alongside the slower, slender-delta HP115, before being retired and moved to the Museum of Flight at East Fortune in 1975. *British Aircraft Corporation*

The Henley/Hotspur dilemma

Kenneth E. Wixey

As the retreating British and French forces fought bitterly against the advancing German Wehrmacht in the grim days of 1940 prior to the Dunkirk evacuation, one weapon conspicuous by its absence, which could have provided some relief and support to Allied ground troops, was a fast ground-attack aircraft — one to fulfil the role which today is described as close air support. Unfortunately the only available type even remotely capable of undertaking this mission was the Fairey Battle, a virtually defenceless light bomber, too slow and far too vulnerable for ground attack missions. By 1940 these machines had become obsolete, but were nevertheless flown by their gallant crews against impossible odds, often on suicidal attacks. Yet had it not been for a sudden change of policy at the British Air Ministry in 1938, the RAF might well have possessed an aircraft quite capable of the fast moving close-support role when such a type was required during 1940.

Early in 1934, the Air Ministry had issued Specification P4/34 calling for a light bomber with the ability to operate as a tactical support aircraft. The type was to be stressed for dive-bombing, and a top speed of 300mph was envisaged. In response to these requirements, prototypes were produced by Fairey Aviation and Hawker Aircraft Ltd. The Fairey design by Marcel Lobelle was known as the P4/34 'Unnamed Bomber', two prototypes — K5099 and K7555, being produced. This design later formed a basis for development of the Fulmar two-seat naval fighter.

Below: Hawker Henley prototype K5115, which made its first flight from Brooklands airfield, Weybridge on 10 March 1937. The aircraft was later used as a flying test-bed on engine development work.
Unless otherwise credited, all photographs courtesy Military Aircraft Photographs

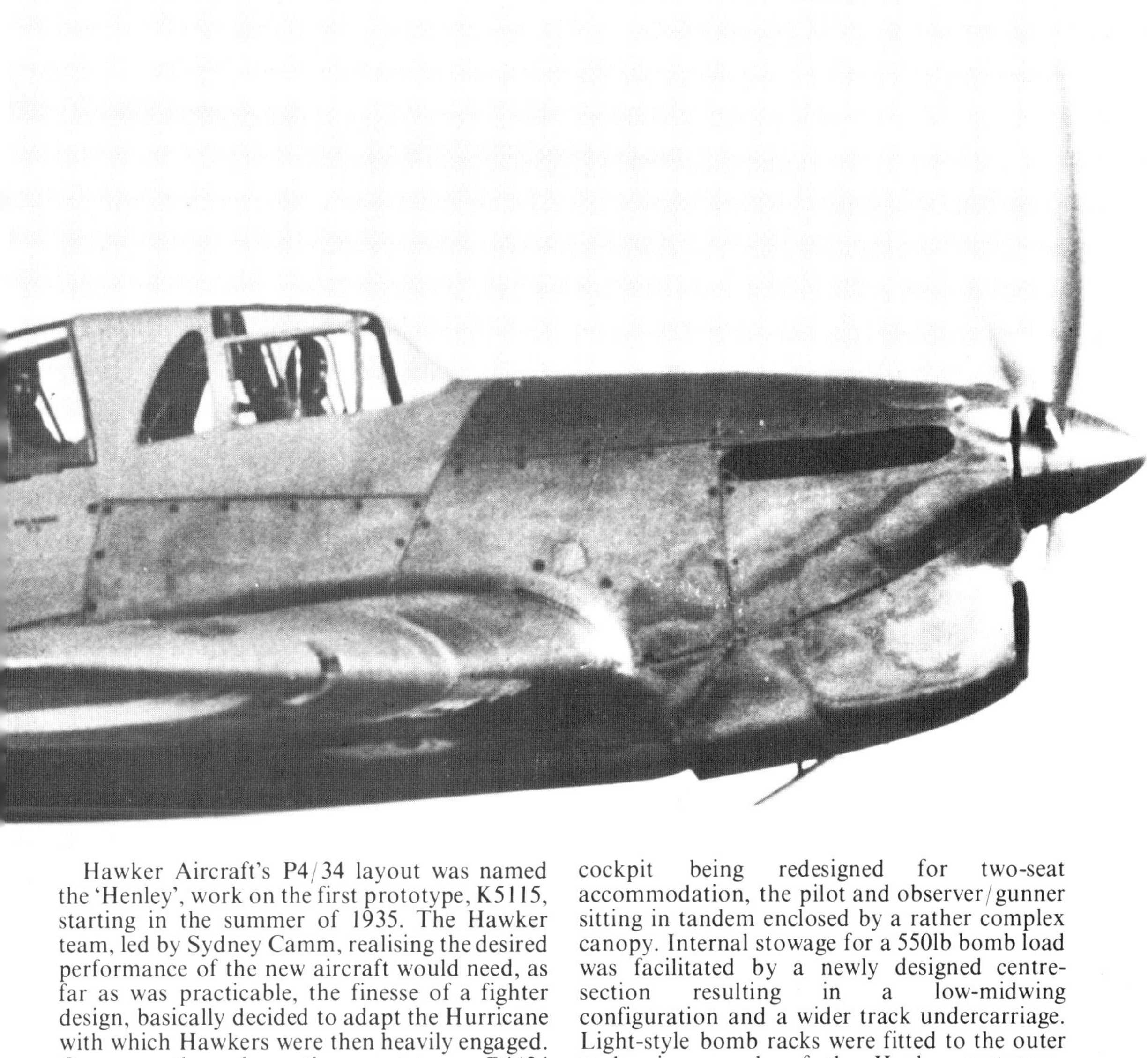

Hawker Aircraft's P4/34 layout was named the 'Henley', work on the first prototype, K5115, starting in the summer of 1935. The Hawker team, led by Sydney Camm, realising the desired performance of the new aircraft would need, as far as was practicable, the finesse of a fighter design, basically decided to adapt the Hurricane with which Hawkers were then heavily engaged. Consequently when the prototype P4/34 Henley appeared the aircraft bore a marked resemblance to the 'Hurri'. The similarity was hardly surprising since to simplify the production programme, the Hurricane and Henley outer wing panels and tailplanes were constructed on identical jigs. Major alterations which resulted in the Henley were obvious, the cockpit being redesigned for two-seat accommodation, the pilot and observer/gunner sitting in tandem enclosed by a rather complex canopy. Internal stowage for a 550lb bomb load was facilitated by a newly designed centre-section resulting in a low-midwing configuration and a wider track undercarriage. Light-style bomb racks were fitted to the outer underwing panels of the Henley prototype, K5115, on which it was intended to carry eight 25lb bombs. Defensive armament comprised a wing-mounted Vickers Mk V machine-gun and a 0.303in Lewis machine-gun in the rear cockpit. Of all-metal construction with fabric covering, K5115 made its first flight from Brooklands on 10 March 1937, powered by a Rolls-Royce

Merlin 'F' liquid-cooled in-line engine driving a three-blade Hamilton hydromatic airscrew. Later a 1,030hp Merlin I power-plant was installed while metal stressed-skin wing surfaces replaced the fabric covering. Thus modified, K5115 flew on 20 August 1937, and in the same year was displayed at the RAF Hendon Air Pageant where, in all-silver finish, it stood in the 'new types' enclosure.

Extensive trials were carried out with the new Henley, including a series of spinning and dive tests from which the machine emerged with few vices. In fact test reports indicated that the Henley was ideal for dive-bombing, and showed promise of an excellent close-support potential.

In the event, decisions being taken at the Air Ministry over-shadowed the P4/34 type's progress, and despite a favourable response during its trials, Hawker's attack-bomber was destined never to become a combat aircraft. A ministerial change of policy regarding the deployment of light-weight close-support aircraft decreed that production versions of the Henley were to be relegated to target-towing duties! Whether or not the ministers responsible were correct in their decision has remained a matter for conjecture, but at the time, certain other factors weighed heavily against acceptance of the Henley for its intended light attack-bomber role.

Above: The second prototype Hawker Henley, K7554, converted as the prototype TT Mk III — the aircraft is shown prior to the application of a camouflage paint scheme.

Above right: One of the Gloster Aircraft Co-built Henleys, L3276. *Imperial War Museum*

British officials had already become rather sceptical of the merits of ground-attack aircraft after studying the vulnerability of the type during the Spanish Civil War, especially when the contemporary advanced fighters appeared on the scene. But an even greater threat to the Henley manifested itself in the limited supply of constant-speed propellers. To perform effectively in the close-support role, the Henley would require this type of airscrew, and in the late 1930s they were being allotted to the urgently needed Hurricanes and Spitfires then in production under the RAF expansion scheme. An order for two or three hundred Henley bombers would have meant a contract for an equal quantity of constant-speed airscrews, and there just were not enough available. Nevertheless there is no denying the Henley in its intended role could have made a very useful contribution indeed in blunting the

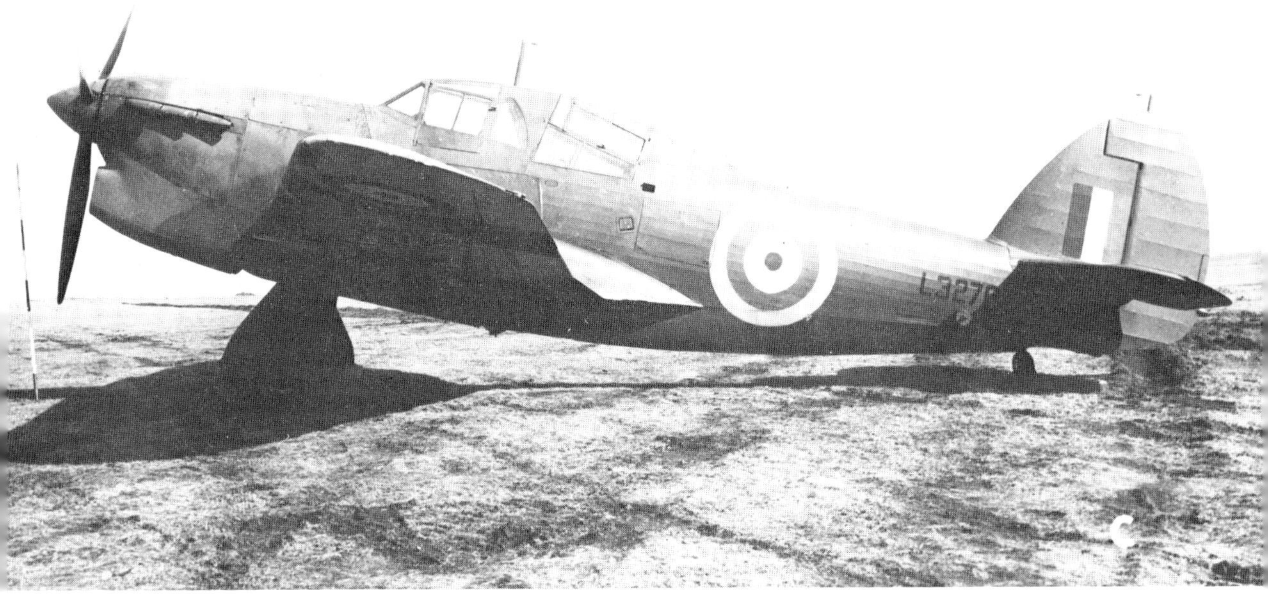

May-June 1940 blitzkreig on France and the Low Countries.

The second prototype Henley, K7554, appeared in 1938, also as a close-support light bomber, the first flight being made from Brooklands on 26 May. However, the decision of the Air Ministry to cancel the requirement embodied in the type was finalised by a stipulation that all production Henleys should be built as target tugs. At the termination of its initial trials period, therefore, the second prototype was transferred to the Gloster Aircraft Company Ltd at Hucclecote, Glos (by then a well established member of the Hawker Siddeley Group) for conversion into the target towing MkIII, and it duly became the prototype Henley TTIII. The principal modification involved in the conversion to the new role was a windmill type mechanism mounted horizontally on the port side of the rear cockpit. In flight this device was rotated by the slipstream, and also had the capability to wind in the target after use.

During the late 1930s, target towing aircraft in RAF service were mainly ageing biplane types like the Fairey Gordon and Westland Wallace, but with the advent of more advanced fighters it was obvious that a faster type of aircraft was required to tow the drogue targets. The Air Ministry decided the Henley would provide an ideal monoplane substitute for the old biplanes, and consequently 200 TTIIIs were ordered, this being the residue of an original contract for 350 production Henleys. Hawker Aircraft Ltd, by then heavily involved with Hurricane production, placed responsibility for the Henley contract with the Gloster Aircraft Co Ltd. The complete batch of production Henleys was built at Hucclecote between October 1938 and September 1940, their serial numbers being in the sequence L3243 — L3442 en bloc. Meanwhile the prototype Henley, K5115, was retained at Hawkers for development purposes where it was known as the MkI. However, in 1939, Rolls-Royce Aero Engines requested modifications to be carried out on the aircraft in order that it could be used as a flying test-bed for the Vulture engine; this was agreed, and the machine was duly sent in suitably modified form to Rolls-Royce at Hucknall.

The second prototype Henley, K7554, was sometimes referred to as the MkII, but in its eventual capacity as the prototype target tug conversion it was officially known as the MkIII. This aircraft later appeared in camouflaged upper surfaces with the standard target tug undersurface of black and yellow dazzle stripes. Production Henleys employed as test-beds included L3302 (Rolls-Royce Vulture), used as a back up machine for K5115 when the Vulture proved exceptionally troublesome under test conditions, L3414 (Rolls-Royce Griffon II), this Henley contributing greatly in development of the Fairey Firefly naval aircraft, and L3441, employed as a specially tropicalised version to test equipment for use in desert regions.

During the second half of 1939, Henleys began entering service with the RAF appearing at various gunnery schools including those at Barrow, Squires Gate and Millom. For air-to-air target tug work the Henley TTIIIs usually towed a MkIII drogue, a fairly small target with which it could attain a speed of approximately 265mph — although around 275mph was possible in short spurts. However, the hard pressed Rolls-Royce Merlin engines began to

Below: Another view of the Henley second prototype, K7554, seen after its modification as the forerunner of the target-towing Mk III — note the windmill mechanism mounted outboard of the rear cockpit. *Hawker Siddeley Aviation*

show signs of excessive wear with the result that the towing speed of all Henley TTIIIs was limited to 220mph. This was a very unrealistic speed for the passage of the aerial targets upon which budding young fighter pilots were expected to practise their attacks, and was certainly not representative of the speeds being achieved by enemy aircraft than in operation. The inevitable result was a gradual withdrawal of the Henleys from air-to-air target towing duties, and their transfer to Anti-Aircraft Co-operation units, including Nos 639 and 695 Squadrons.

The Henleys were now faced with the problem of towing the larger type drogues necessary for anti-aircraft work, and it was found that unless full throttle was applied the TTIIIs had great difficulty in maintaining even 200mph. This created further difficulties as a consequence of the slow speeds of the Henley tugs was the insufficient cooling, and resultant overheating of their Merlin engines. Power-plant failures became a common occurrence affecting the struggling TTIIIs, and some idea of the rate of attrition can be deduced from the fact that one unit alone, No 1 AACU, lost nine of its Henleys during 1941-42 due to crashes and forced landings caused by engine failures. These machines were L3243; L3298; L3395; L3265; L3363; L3251; L3378; L3328 and L3399. Two other Henleys known to have suffered the same fate in 1943 were L3420 (crashed at Farnborough) and L3331 (force landed near Great Yarmouth).

The other units which flew Henleys during the early war years were Nos 1, 5 and 10 Bombing and Gunnery Schools and No 1611 Flight. By June 1942, however, there were less than 40 serviceable Henleys available, but by then they were being replaced by Boulton Paul Defiant two-seat fighters, which had been converted as target tugs, and by the new Miles Martinat tugs. At least two Henleys are known to have later been employed as trials aircraft, L3247 going to Martlesham Heath and L3252 to the RAF at Farnborough.

The engines fitted to the production Henleys varied slightly, the first 100 machines having the 1,030hp Rolls-Royce Merlin II while the second 100 TTIIIs were fitted with the Merlin III. All 200 production aircraft were provided with three-blade de Havilland controllable-pitch airscrews.

An unusual derivative of the Henley evolved in prototype form only, and was built by Hawkers in response to Air Ministry Specification F9/35, which was issued in the autumn of 1935. This called for a two-seat fighter with the main armament concentrated in a power-operated turret.

When this specification was presented, the Hawker Demon two-seat biplane fighter was still in RAF squadron service. Most of the Demons were eventually equipped with a Frazer-Nash hydraulically operated gun turret in which the gunner was protected in the rear by a 'lobster-back' shield. Known as the 'Turret Demon' this version was built under contract by Boulton Paul Aircraft Ltd at Wolverhampton, and it was envisaged the new fighter resulting from Specification F9/35 would provide the Demon replacement. Stipulations within F9/35 demanded a design which would have a performance on a par with any contemporary fighter, including single-seaters, that it would be capable of good manoeuvrability, feature a fuel capacity allowing standing patrols to be undertaken, and aerodynamically clean. In addition, as it was considered that the best attacking position for a turret-equipped fighter was from below an enemy bomber formation, it was required that the new fighter's power-operated turret should be capable of an effective field of fire through 360° in azimuth. Considering the inevitable weight and drag factor of the turret, Specification F9/35 appeared to be a tall order for a fighter, but even so work on the new design began in the spring of 1936, and four well-known aircraft manufacturers — Armstrong Whitworth, Boulton Paul, Bristols and Hawkers — submitted proposals pursuant to the requirement.

Below: A sporty attitude for a Henley TTIII and one rather more appropriate to the ground attack role originally envisaged for the design.

Below right: The sole example of the proposed 4-gun turret armed version of the Henley, the Hawker Hotspur, which was built in response to Spec F9/35. The requirement was met by the Boulton-Paul Defiant.

The Armstrong Whitworth design, a twin-engined low-wing monoplane with a 39ft wing span and known simply as the AW F9/35, was dropped at an early stage. The machine was to have been powered by two Armstrong Siddeley Terrier engines, the power-operated turret beng situated in a mid-upper position. The Bristol Aeroplane Co Ltd based the interpretation of F9/35 on its Type 146 monoplane, a single-seat fighter, and on the Type 148 army co-operation two-seat monoplane. The result was the proposed Type 147, which was to incorporate a turret with a rotating seat for the gunner, the armament comprising four 0.303in Browning machine-guns. Boulton Paul Aircraft Ltd profferred the P82, later to be named the Defiant, and eventual winner of the contract and a production order.

Meanwhile Hawker Aircraft Ltd built their Henley offshoot and named it the Hotspur. The machine was in fact basically a Henley with a redesigned cockpit canopy, revised rear fuselage, modified tailplane contours and a power-operated rear turret, which in the event materialised as a wooden 'mock-up' only. Owing to heavy commitments with the Hurricane, Hawkers were seriously delayed with their Hotspur development programme, the single prototype, K8309, never in fact flying at its all-up weight. The first flight of the Hotspur did not take place until 14 June 1938, and as Boulton Paul had flown their P82 Defiant contender the previous August as well as won an Air Ministry production order four months prior to the Hotspur's first flight, it was a foregone conclusion that the Hotspur would not be accepted. The Hotspur actually proved faster than its rival during flight testing and was reported to handle well, although it should be realised K8309 flew with only ballast and the wooden mock-up turret. Once it had been decided there was no viable prospect for the Hotspur, it was modified by having the turret removed and the cockpit revised, the gunner's position being enclosed by a fairing incorporating a glazed section for an observer. K8309 was then used by Hawkers to test various equipment in connection with the development of the Henley light bomber until that programme itself was abandoned. Afterwards the prototype Hotspur was delivered to the RAF at Farnborough, where it was employed as a trials aircraft between 1939 and 1942, and officially known as Experimental Aeroplane No 155.

Although only the single Hotspur was built, an order for 389 production machines (L3643 — L4031) had been placed by the Air Ministry, the complete batch intended as a production contract for A. V. Roe & Co Ltd, but this was

quickly rescinded. In the event the whole concept of the turret fighter did not live up to expectations, a fact proved later by the disastrous losses suffered by the Defiant squadrons once the *Luftwaffe* pilots realised the vulnerability of the type. Nonetheless, once the Defiant was taken off daylight operations to become an AI radar equipped night-fighter in the winter of 1940-41 when it retrieved some of the reputation it lost in the Battle of Britain. Nor was the design concept enhanced by the Blackburn Roc (developed from the Skua fighter/dive-bomber) turret fighter's lack of any creditable performance which would have been beneficial to the Fleet Air Arm if employed in its

Below: Another view of the Hotspur prototype with its wooden mock-up rear turret.

intended role. Rocs served only a short time with two FAA units, Nos 801 and 806 Squadrons, both shore-based, and were soon relegated to training and target towing duties. Had the Hawker Hotspur been produced, it too would in all probability have suffered the same fate as the Defiant and Roc, both victims of a concept in aerial warfare doomed to failure once the faster single-seat fighters had the measure of their turreted fighter opponents.

Hawker Henley TTIII
Type: Two-seat target-tug
Powerplant: One 1,030hp Rolls-Royce Merlin II or III liquid-cooled in-line engine
Span: 47ft 10.5in
Length: 36ft 5in
Height: 14ft 7.5in
Weight: 6,010lb (empty)
8,480lb (loaded)
Max Speed: 272mph at 17,000ft (towing air-to-air drogue)
200mph (towing AACU drogue)
Climb rate: 1,150ft/min
Service ceiling: 27,000ft
*Range:*950 miles
Armament: None fitted on target-tug model

Hawker Hotspur
Type: Two-seat interceptor turret fighter
Powerplant: One 1,025hp Rolls-Royce Merlin II liquid-cooled in-line engine.
Span: 47ft 10in
Length: 36ft 1.5in
Height: 14ft 4in
Weight: 5,800lb (empty)
7,650lb (loaded)
Max speed: 316mph at 15,800ft
Climb rate: 15,000ft in 10,5min
Service ceiling: 28,000ft
Armament: One fixed forward-firing 0.303in Vickers machine-gun mounted in port side of nose synchronised to fire through the propeller arc (rovisional) Four 0.303in Browning machine-guns housed ina semi-power-operated turret (Boulton Paul-built) fitted immediately behind cockpit (proposed but only wooden 'mock-up' installed with armament ballast).

Acknowledgements
The author wishes to thank Mr R. Simpson (Dept of Archives/Aviation Records, RAF Museum, Hendon) and British Aerospace, Kingston-upon-Thames, for their assistance in the preparation of this article.

The 'Red Arrows' new era

Roger Hoefling

Right: The 1980 'Red Arrows' and their new aircraft seen en-route from the BAe airfield at Bitteswell, Leics to RAF Kemble on 15 November 1979 and, inset, a new logo produced by the manufacturer to mark the team's re-equipment with Hawk T1s. *BAe Kingston*

Below: The 'Red Arrows' in Diamond Nine formation during a Gnat T1 era display. *Andrew March*

One of the Royal Air Force Benevolent Fund's Christmas cards last year was entitled 'The Red Arrows — Sunset of the Gnat', an event that came in fact in September 1979. At close to 40,000 it was the largest crowd of recent years at RAF St Athan's Battle of Britain At-Home Day on 15 September that saw the last public display by the 'Red Arrows' on Gnats. Arriving from the day's other display at RAF Abingdon, the finale was in perfect weather but the Gnat did not go without a little reluctance. The team, having had to spend most of the season flying only eight aircraft due to the unfortunate illness of Flt Lt Tim Curley, bowed out with only seven. One of the aircraft had to make a precautionary departure from the formation about one third of the way through the sequence, later landing safely with the rest of the team. It meant the team manager having to give up his machine to enable eight refuelled Gnats to taxi-out past their last public audience for a take-off to RAF Valley. Hankerchiefs were much in evidence inside the barrier and not all were for waving. Indeed, it is reported that one very high-ranking RAF officer was moved to observe, 'It's only the aircraft that are going, we're not shooting the pilots!'

The last apperance of all came later that afternoon in front of a specially-invited audience at RAF Valley; the former home of the Gnat in RAF service. The next day, Sunday, the aircraft returned to their base at RAF Kemble, so ending a 15-year career for the Gnat as the mount of the 'Red Arrows'. Now equivalent to a standard RAF squadron and forming part of the Central Flying School, the team formed on the type at RAF Fairford in 1965. Flying seven aircraft in display, they were led by Flt Lt Lee Jones who the previous year had led the 'Yellowjacks', five appropriately-coloured Gnats from No 4 Flying Training School at

Valley. The Service's official aerobatic team in 1964, however, was the 'Red Pelicans' using six Jet Provost T4s and they were the first Central Flying School team to have that leading role. In combining something of both those teams, therefore, the 'Red Arrows' also acknowledged in their chosen name their predecessors of 1957-1960, the 'Black Arrows' of No 111 Squadron.

In their first season, the 'Red Arrows' gave 65 performances; the 1,000th was reached on 26 June 1977 at the International Air Tattoo at Greenham Common while the grand total with the Gnats came to 1,292 official displays — claimed as a world record on one aircraft type. Ninety per cent of that performance total was given over the UK, the remainder through Europe, the Middle East and North America — 18 overseas countries in all. Presenting the team to an annual live audience estimated at 3.5 million people, it is a record that, while for a number of reasons there can never be a world's 'best' aerobatic team, has shown the 'Red Arrows' to be the world's most consistent team by their standard through the range of display conditions and weather.

It is against the background of that record that the 1980 season has started a new era for the 'Red Arrows' when they displayed for the first time on the Gnat's successor, the Hawk. Heralding this came the formal hand-over ceremony of the team's ninth such aircraft at Bitteswell on 15 November 1979 with the tenth, reserve, machine then being due at the end of that month.

On that occasion it was the inhospitable weather that denied the team a chance to show those on the ground all nine aircraft in formation but the accompanying photographs show the most obvious changes worn by the new type. The colour scheme has been developed from that gradually evolved on the Gnat; overall 'rocket Red', with a low wing now allowing full extension of the white cheat line aft, broadening to sweep up and form the central stripe of the fin and rudder flash. The effect is to reduce the humped-back appearance of the Hawk. Gone, for the moment anyway at the start of the training programme for the 1980 season, were

Right: Bomb-burst by a seven aircraft 'Red Arrows' formation at RAF Benson in September 1969. *Peter R. March*

Below right: Gnat T1s of the 'Red Arrows' taking off at Bournemouth-Hurn Airport in July 1978, the team's penultimate season with the aircraft. *Peter R. March*

Below: The 'Red Arrows' predecessors, the 'Yellowjacks' at RAF Little Rissington with their yellow-painted Gnat T1s in August 1964. *Peter R. March*

ROYAL AIR FORCE

Above: The 'Arrows' displaying at Halfpenny Green in September 1969 and, very unusually, with underwing fuel tanks fitted to the Gnats. *Peter R. March*

Left: The logbook of the ninth 'Red Arrows' Hawk T1, XX266, is accepted by Air Cdre Dennis Allison, Commandant of the Central Flying School, during the Handover ceremony at Bitteswell on 15 November 1979: on the right is Sqn Ldr Brian Hoskins, the team's leader. *BAe Kingston*

Top right: The ninth aircraft, XX266, on roll-out at Bitteswell on 15 November 1979. *Martin Horseman*

Above right: All nine 'Red Arrows' Hawk T1s on the flight line at Bitteswell prior to their departure for Kemble later the same day. *Martin Horseman*

the Union Flag from the fin, the CFS crest and underwing serial numbers, while the prominent 'Royal Air Force' legend on the nose of the Gnats has re-appeared, but more subdued in blue and within the cheat line.

Airborne, however, it can be seen that the underside of the aircraft is being exploited by the team for the first time. A red and white arrowhead now appears beneath the fuselage and wings while upper wing surfaces remain plain red.

The painting of the aircraft was the work of BAe personnel at Bitteswell. For the past ten years the establishment has provided major servicing support for the team's Gnats and will continue similarly with the Hawk. This involvement has been more than cosmetic, however, Bitteswell being responsible for most of the task of preparing the otherwise basic Hawk T1 to the team's requirements. A major item is the smoke generation system. Unlike the Gnat which carried internally the diesel fuel and red and blue dyes used to produce smoke, each Hawk will utilise a modified 30mm Aden gun pod converted as a three-bay tank, and fixed to the centre-line station. Internal piping will lead

Above: 'Red Arrows' Hawk T1 trio lifting off from Bitteswell on a cold and wet 15 November 1979 for their flight to Kemble.
Martin Horseman

through the fuselage to exhaust as three separate vents above the jetpipe. Other differences encompass improved brakes — the Hawk in RAF service not using a brake parachute; better hydraulic system access and a change in the stand-by radio. To come is the uprated powerplant, the Adour-56 of 5,700lb st in place of the standard Mk 151 of 5,340lb st.

Some of the these modifications were yet to be completed at the time of the handover so until the beginning of 1980 the team only had six Hawks with which to pratice; the first was delivered in August 1979. Thus while only one half or side of some of the main formations had been flown by late 1979, Sqn Ldr Brian Hoskins, team leader for a second year in 1980, already regarded the aircraft as 'the best for this particular role' and aerodynamically better than its predecessor. In detail, this is exemplified by the better balance of the controls, the aircraft holding its own axis very well in the roll and being more stable in formation: the Hawk allows tighter positioning than the Gnat in some manoeuvres. Although the new degree of wing sweepback will make some formations look different and the rolling properties of the Hawk may well come to the fore, it seems unlikely that the 'Red Arrows' 1980 display sequence will exhibit any major changes from that of last year.

It is in more than its aerodynamics that the Hawk is an improvement over the Gnat, for hardly less telling on the display scene is the promise of its higher fuel economy and reduced servicing demands. Sqn Ldr Hoskins has suggested a fuel saving of up to 40% on Gnat operation while new features such as pressure refuelling and an internal starter combined in an aircraft designed anyway to need less servicing that the Gnat or Hunter mean improved turnround times. Together, these factors will make possible a more intensive display programme than hitherto or, at least, one that could be conducted at ranges greater than the present maximum of 35 miles from a base.

In fact, the number of displays in the first year of the Hawk will be around 110; the total for

1979 in spite of bad weather was 123. Limiting factors to some extent will continue to be the need to replenish the smoke tanks after each performance, a process that can take the better part of hour with the pod not being exchangeable, as well as the need for the team manager and commentator, Sqn Ldr Ray Thilthorpe, to position for each display ahead of the team. Very important, though, is the wish to allow the groundcrew and Support Sqadron a full opportunity to assimilate the new aircraft before embarking on a more ambitious programme.

The Hawk's record in the RAF bodes well for its new career, however. By mid-November 1979, 109 out of a total order of 175 aircraft had been delivered: since delivery of the first examples in November 1976, a total of 40,000 flying hours has been amassed and the total for all versions of the Adour engine has exceeded 600,000 hours. The unblemished safety record of the Hawk was described at the Bitteswell handover as 'impeccable and unprecendented'.

That three-year interval between the Service taking its first Hawks and the 'Red Arrows' re-equipping is the same as that for the Gnat. The latter though was at the end of its development — the prototype Gnat single-seater first flew in 1955, the Midge the year before — whereas it is hoped that the Hawk is but at the beginning. It may be the first Kingston-designed trainer since the Tomtit of 1928 but it has the wider potential of the light-strike role. The three export orders so far received are hoped to be only the first of many. With this in mind, Sqn Ldr Hoskins lists the purpose of the 'Red Arrows' as threefold: to promote recruiting for the Services in general and the RAF in particular; to demonstrate the pilots' and aircraft's skills and capabilities and, finally, to promote the aeroplane and the British aerospace industry.

Above: The large arrow featured on the underside of the 'Red Arrows' Hawks is illustrated in this view of one of the team's aircraft. *BAe Kingston*

In 1980 that aeroplane may be new but the standards will be the same. In that purpose, even if the 'Diamond Nine' will take some getting used to, those left on the ground would want to wish the 'Red Arrows' and their new mount well.

Below: The 1980 'Red Arrows' team and their aircraft. The team members are, from left to right, Flt Lts Byron Walters, Neal Wharton, Richard Thomas (Deputy Leader), Malcolm Howell, Sqn Ldr Brian Hoskins (Leader), Flt Lts Wyndham Ward, Steve Johnson, Bernie Scott and Tim Watts. *BAe Kingston*

Bottom: The colour scheme adopted for the 'Red Arrows' Hawk T1s as portrayed by XX253. *BAe Kingston*

ROYAL AIR FORCE

The Hanriot HD-1

R. A. Nicholls

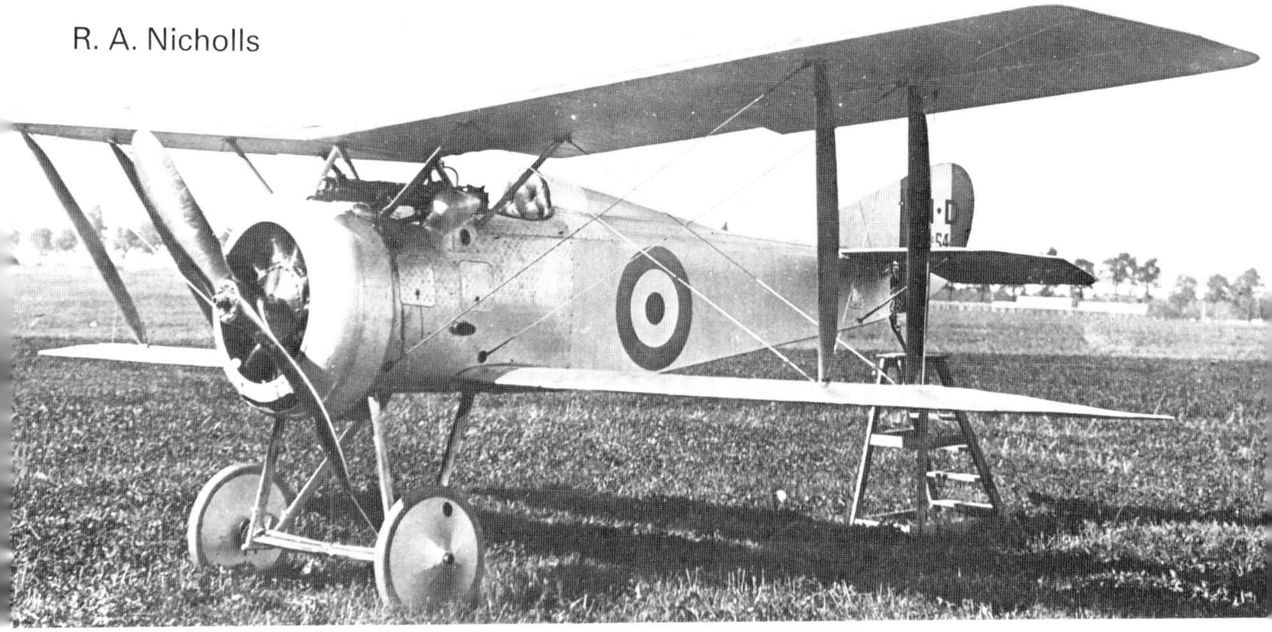

Above: An early French-built machine, s/n HD-54. This aircraft would appear to be one of the initial batch built for the *CAM* in the Billancourt factory, and seen in France before delivery. *Imperial War Museum*

Rene Hanriot, a pioneer French aircraft builder and designer, whose designs in the years 1910 to 1913 had been noted for their stability, ease of handling, and pleasing lines, turned his attention to a new project at the beginning of 1916. After retiring from the aviation scene in 1913, Hanriot had returned to aircraft building at the start of the Great War, building a new factory at Billancourt, France, where his company produced Sopwith 1½-Strutters under licence.

Hanriot was joined at Billancourt by designer Pierre Dupont, and together they set about designing and building a replacement for the Nieuport 11 scout aircraft, which was then in widespread service with the Allies. Despite the Nieuport 11's initial success in the hands of pilots such as Bishop and Nungesser, by 1916 it was clear that the lower mainplane lacked the strength to stand up to the rigours of continual aerial fighting over the European battlefields; furthermore, by that time its performance was markedly inferior to many of its contemporaries, both friend and foe. Clearly it was time for a replacement aircraft, and the Hanriot/Dupont team had high hopes that their design would be the one to find favour with the Allied air arms.

The design on which Hanriot and Dupont pinned their hopes was the Hanriot HD-1, which appeared in mid-1916, a single-seat fighter/scout in the classic mould with a wing span of 8.7m and 5.85m long. Perfectly proportioned, the initial impression was of a clean, diminutive aircraft, with a marked lack of external bracing wires. The HD-1 looked every inch a winner, and the makers had good reason to be confident of substantial orders.

The powerplant selected was the 110hp version of the Le Rhone 9J rotary engine,

Left: The Hanriot HD-1, s/n HD-75, now in the RAF Museum at Hendon seen in its pristine post-repaint condition at the Museum's Restoration Centre at Cardington — the aircraft has been finished in the colours of *1e Escadrille, Aviation Militaire Belge. R. A Nicholls*

Above: Although the Le Rhone 9JB was employed on most HD-1s, other rotary engines were experimented with including the 130hp Clerget fitted here to an *AMB* aircraft, HD-61. Note also the modified fin outline and addition of a horn balance to the rudder. *Imperial War Museum*

performance of the Le Rhone series of engines having been proven and their reliability firmly established in service. The result was a top speed of 177km/h coupled with a service ceiling of 6,000 metres and an endurance of 2½hr, which allowed the HD-1 to meet most of its potential adversaries on equal terms, and in many cases with a positive advantage. This was later changed and various more powerful versions were fitted, up to the 170hp Le Rhone 9R, the majority employing the 120hp 9Jb. The use of the 9Jb version on most of the production aircraft increased the top speed to 184 km/h, and gave a slight improvement in manoeuverability and response.

When the flying trials were undertaken the HD-1 proved to be the epitome of that hackneyed axiom, beloved of aviators the world over, 'if it looks right, it flies right'. A marked resemblance to the Sopwith Pup reflected Hanriot's involvement in the production of Sopwith aircraft, and showed that his ideas had been influenced by the association. The flying trials only confirmed what Hanriot and Dupont were already confident of; the HD-1 was a highly commendable aircraft, inherently stable but with excellent manoeuverability, and highly responsive to the movement of the flying controls. The stability and manoeuverability were due in no small part to the gyroscopic effect and torque reaction of the Le Rhone rotary engine, in which the crankshaft remained stationery while the cylinders and crankcase, to which the propeller was fixed, rotated around it. In the hands of an experienced pilot, the torque reaction could be used to great advantage in a dog-fight to out-turn another aircraft and get on its tail. Possessing all the qualities which endear an aircraft, particularly a fighter, to a pilot, the future looked bright indeed for the HD-1.

Hanriot's high hopes had received a setback when the French themselves ordered the Spad VII as a replacement for their Nieuports. Foreign interest remained high, however, and the first order came from Italy, where the *Corpo Aeronautico Militaire* had need of a replacement for its Nieuports. After extensive trials, the Italians placed an order for a total of 1,700 machines, although this was later reduced, only 831 being delivered. Apart from a small

Above: An early production machine in France. Note the offset position of the Vickers gun, later centralised by both the *CAM* and the *AMB*: this led to a marked improvement in the gunnery of the pilots of both services. *Jean Noël, via J. M. Bruce*

batch of French-built machines, the Italian HD-1's were licence-built by Nieuport-Macchi at their Varese factory in Italy, work commencing in November 1916. First deliveries to training units followed by mid-1917, and in August of that year the first *CAM* unit became operational on the HD-1. This was the *76a Squadriglia,* and the type rapidly established itself as the standard fighter in *CAM* service, eventually equipping 16 out of a total complement of 18 fighter squadrons and being the most widely-used aircraft in Italian service for the remainder of the war and beyond. In early 1918, as a result of increasingly frequent Austrian air raids on the naval base of Venice, 12 of the *CAM's* HD-1s were used to form the basis of the *241a Squadriglia*, a newly-formed unit under the command of the Italian Navy and manned by a mixture of *CAM* and Navy personnel; this unit was assigned to the task of local air defence of the naval base, but also undertook fleet escort duties and patrols. The Italian HD-1's saw service in Albania and Macedonia as well as in Italy itself, and a few were still in service when the *CAM* was integrated into the newly-formed *Regia Aeronautica* in 1923.

Apart from the *CAM* the only other user of the HD-1 in any quantity was the *Aviation Militaire Belge,* which received a total of 125, all French-built. The HD-1 entered service with the AMB's 1 Squadron at Les Moeres on 22 August August 1917, the order having been placed two months previously. The HD-1s of the *AMB* were the only examples of the type to see service on the Western Front. So popular was the HD-1, and so successful were the Belgian pilots who flew it in combat, that when in early 1918 Sopwith Camels were offered to the *AMB* as possible HD-1 replacements, the views of the pilots were taken into account, and the Camel supplemented the HD-1 in Belgian service rather than replacing it. After the war the HD-1 remained in *AMB* service, albeit in decreasing numbers, until 1926.

Armaments on the HD-1 consisted of a single 0.303in Vickers machine gun mounted on the port side of the upper fuselage decking, firing forwards through the propeller by means of

Above: HD-78, minus armament, is preserved in the Belgian Army Museum, Brussels. This view shows the high degree of stagger between the upper and lower mainplanes.
R. A. Nicholls

a Constantinesco hydraulic synchroniser. Practical experience led the *CAM* to modify the gun installations on their HD-1s by moving the gun onto the fuselage centreline, thus considerably easing problems of sighting for the pilot, and this modification was also incorporated by the *AMB* on their machines. The single fixed gun was rather unusual at a time when most of the HD-1's contemporaries were sporting two forward-firing machine guns, but trials with a twin Vickers installation showed that this increase in firepower could only be obtained at the cost of a marked drop in performance, and consequently this idea was not proceeded with, firepower at that time taking second place to an aircraft's flying qualities.

In France the HD-1 was very much overshadowed by the Spad VII and XII, and no French order was forthcoming until 1918, when the naval *Service Aeronautique* placed an order for a small number for use as shipboard fighters. The last sale of the HD-1 was in 1921 when the Swiss *Militar-Flugwesens* bought a batch of 16.

If it appears from all this that the HD-1 did not achieve the full measure of success which it deserved, then Hanriot's next design fared infinitely worse. The HD-2, which appeared in 1918, was basically a float-plane version of the HD-1. Fitted with twin floats, and with an increase in fin and rudder area to compensate, it was armed with two fixed 0.303in Vickers machine guns. The US Navy bought 10 for use as station defence fighters at their naval facilities on the French coast, but these were later taken to the USA, where they were converted for use as land-planes.

Although the HD-1 was not the most widely-used of First World War fighter/scouts, those who flew it were full of praise for its qualities and were loathe to transfer to other types; if not the most successful it was certainly one of the most popular. Almost completely ignored in France, it was left to the Italians and Belgians to prove the worth of the aircraft, and this they did in no small measure. In the hands of Belgian pilots like Coppens and Meulemeester the HD-1 proved itself a true thoroughbred acquitting itself honourably and making a very significant contribution to the Allied effort on the Western

Above: Switzerland bought 16 HD-1s for the *Militar-Flugwesens* in 1921 and the aircraft, which carried the s/nos 651-666, operated for many years at Dubendorf: 653, seen here at Dubendorf, is now preserved in the Swiss Transport Museum at Lucerne.
Swiss Transport Museum, via J. M. Bruce

Left: One of a number of HD-1s sold off by the *AMB* was HD-75, pictured here at Evere, Belgium in 1923 after assuming its civil identity. It is this machine, bought by Richard Shuttleworth in 1935 and later donated to the RAF Museum by a subsequent US owner, Mr Marvin Hand, which is now on show at Hendon.
A. Twycross, via J. M. Bruce

Below left: Although Charter Nungesser did not fly the type operationally, his wartime insignia was applied to 5934 for the post WW1 tour of the US. *Imperial War Museum*

Front. In Italian service the HD-1 was every bit as successful, and its most impressive demonstration of its fighting abilities came on 26 December 1917, when, in aerial combat over Istrana, the HD-1s of the *CAM's 6a Gruppo* destroyed 11 German aircraft without loss to themselves. On the basis of its fighting record, and its popularity with those who flew it, the HD-1 can truly claim a place in the roll of the classic fighters of the Great War.

After progress had rendered the HD-1 obsolete as a military aircraft, a number re-appeared in civil markings, their graceful lines and crisp response making them popular with private fliers, many of whom were former First World War pilots.

Today, almost 63 years after the HD-1 first appeared in the war-torn skies over Europe, only five examples remain in existence, all of them in museums. HD-1 s/n 5934, which was taken to the USA by the flamboyant French ace Charles Nungesser in 1923, is preserved in the Air Museum at Ontario, California. This was one of the aircraft used by Nungesser during his barnstorming days in the USA, being flown in mock dog-fights and appearing in at least one film, before Nungesser disappeared without trace during an attempt to fly the Atlantic from East to West in May 1927. The Museum of Transport in Lucerne has on show one of the examples used by the *Militar-Flugwesens,* s/n 653. Italy and Belgium, the major users of the HD-1, each have one example preserved, the Belgian machine being shown in the markings of *1e Escadrille* of the *AMB,* representing the aircraft flown by Lt Jan Olieslagers in 1917. Although Olieslagers' official tally of victories was only five, it is generally accepted that his true score was very much higher — his combats took place mostly behind the German lines, where ground confirmation of a victory was not usually possible. The fifth and last surviving

Left: HD-78 representing the aircraft flown by 2-Lt Jan Olieslagers of the *AMB* during 1917-1918 and now in the Belgian Army Museum at Brussels. *R. A. Nicholls*

Right, below, and below left: Three views of HD-75 now in the RAF Museum at Hendon, and variously showing the outward slope of the interplane struts, the marked dihedral of the upper mainplane, and the later central position of the Vickers gun. *All R. A. Nichols*

HD-1 is the ex-Belgian aircraft HD-75, which took up residence at the RAF Museum, Hendon, in December 1979 and was featured in its own right in a recent issue of *Aircraft Illustrated* (February 1980).

Unfortunately there is no possibility of us seeing an HD-1 in the air again, and unless an airworthy replica is forthcoming in the future we shall have only these earthbound examples in museums to remind us of this classic fighter/scout which never quite had the success it so richly deserved. In this respect we are fortunate indeed in having such a fine example at Hendon. Gazing at this superb aircraft today, resplendent in its *1e Escadrille* markings, it requires but little imagination to find oneself transported back across the intervening years and picture the scene on an allied airfield in 1917 as the young pilots cast a knowing eye over their mounts before climbing into that cramped and cold cockpit, ready to take off and patrol to the front-line and beyond, hoping to come upon a Fokker, an Albatros, or maybe a Pfalz, trusting to bring them to combat, to triumph, and to live to fight again tomorrow. With just a little more imagination one can convince oneself that at any moment that Le Rhone will cough and come to life as the mechanic swings the polished propeller and, amid an aroma of dope and castor oil, the frail-looking machine will climb purposefully skywards into its natural element, once again to carry out the function for which Hanriot and Dupont designed it all those years ago.

The Lockheed Hudson

the RAF's first operational American aeroplane

Philip J. R. Moyes

Just as the magnificent Hercules become a most valuable asset to the Royal Air Force when it entered service in 1967, so too did that much earlier Lockheed product, the Hudson reconnaissance bomber, prove to be tremendous boon to the RAF following its addition to the inventory way back in 1939. An altogether well-fed looking aeroplane — again like the 'Herky Bird' — the Hudson had the distinction of being the first American aeroplane to serve operationally with the RAF, the sole previous American deliveries for regular use, as opposed to evaluation, being some of the original North American Harvard advanced trainers which, incidentally, were ordered concurrently with the first Hudsons.

The story of the Hudson began in April 1938 — the month after Hitler's troops marched into Prague — when the Air Ministry sent a small team to the USA to look for miltary aircraft, including a general reconnaissance bomber, to supplement the various aircraft being built in Britain under the RAF Expansion Scheme. The team was led by Air Commodore A. T. Harris (later Marshal of the RAF Sir Arthur Harris,

Left: T9326, from the third Hudson I production batch, on test in the US carrying a dummy dorsal turret. Hudsons for the RAF had their bulbous Boulton-Paul turrets installed in the UK.
All photos from the Author's collection

X
17382

Bomber Command's most famous wartime C-in-C) and the first intimation Lockheed received of the proposed trip to Burbank was a telegram from the British air attache in Washington saying that the party would be visiting California aircraft factories within a week. At the time Lockheed had nothing in production except a batch of twin-engined Model 14 Super Electra 11-passenger airliners, so it had to act fast. By working virtually round the clock, it produced a full-scale wooden mock-up of a military version of the Super Electra within five days — just in time to exhibit to the prospective British customers. Performance estimates prepared by chief designer Hall L. Hibbard showed that the projected warplane had sufficient speed and range to become a replacement for RAF Coastal Command's then standard landplane general reconnaissance type, the Avro Anson, and the Air Ministry delegation was greatly impressed. They did, however, suggest modifications which facilitated easier crew movement and re-positioned the navigator in the nose, and to their amazement Lockheed incorporated the mods in a separate nose mock-up in time for further discussions the following day. Actually, the firm produced two new nose mock-ups; the second incorporated its own ideas and this proved to be the one which the British team liked best.

Recalling the episode in his autobiography, *Bomber Offensive,* Sir Arthur Harris wrote: 'As I was well aware that at home we were never able to get a mock-up of any description in less than months, I was entirely convinced that anyone who could produce a mock-up in twenty-fours would indeed make good all his promises — and this Lockheed certainly did.' But first an actual Air Ministry contract had to be obtained, and to this end a Lockheed team, including that legendary research engineer C. L. (Kelly) Johnson — renowned in recent times for designing the remarkable A-11, YF-12 and SR-71 series of Mach 3-capable aircraft — came to London to do some hard selling. The conferences lasted two months, and to work out changes in specifications, Johnson frantically revised blueprints at night in his room at the Mayfair Court Hotel.

Eventually, on 23 June 1938, the Lockheed team's efforts paid off when the Air Ministry ordered 200 examples of the new reconnaissance bomber, which Britain later named the Hudson after early-day explorer Henry Hudson. The ministry also expressed interest in acquiring as many more of the aircraft as could be delivered by December 1939, up to a maximum of 250 at a total cost of $25 million.

The order was announced at the same time as the initial Harvard order, and both orders caused a furore in Britain, as many people deplored the idea of the nation buying foreign-manufactured aircraft for the RAF. However, events in Europe soon proved the contracts to be very wise moves.

In winning the Hudson order, (which, in monetary value, was the largest single order anyone had yet placed with a US aircraft manufacturer) Lockheed also won ridicule from its contemporaries for daring to take on such a big job with the very limited working capital, production facilities and manpower then available. However, the job was done. The first Hudson took to the air on 10 December 1938 and by June of the following year 48 were completed, leaving 202 still to come — in six months! By delegating a substantial amount of parts assembly to Rohr Aircraft in San Diego — a move which marked the US aircraft industry's first step towards major sub-contracting — Lockheed managed to increase production to one Hudson a day, then two. After that it never let up. Its workforce climbed to 7,000 in the period of just one year and the 250th Hudson was rolled out seven and a half weeks ahead of schedule. And, thanks to many more orders, the flow of Hudson-type aircraft, including many for America herself — was to continue until 1943, when the 2,940th and last machine was completed.

Meanwhile, in the spring of 1939, Hudsons began to reach Britain. They came by sea, to Liverpool, and from there they were taken to a Lockheed subsidiary firm at nearby Speke Airport for assembly and testing. Deliveries to RAF Coastal Command commenced in May

Above left: The Hudson — named after early-day explorer Henry Hudson — was derived from the Lockheed 14 Super Electra of 1937 (illustrated), an 11-passenger airliner and the fastest US transport of its day, with a 237mph cruising speed.

Left: At first, Hudsons were shipped to Britain, from both west and east coasts of the US, this batch of Mk 1s being pictured during loading in Long Beach harbour, California, in 1939. The aircraft next to the car on the quayside is N7294.

Left: A Dornier 18 flying boat shot down by a Hudson after a 35-second engagement off the Norwegian coast in April 1940. Another Do18, shot down by two Hudsons on 10 November 1939, was Coastal Command's first *Luftwaffe* 'kill'.

1939 with the handing over of the eighth production Hudson I to No. 224 (General Reconnaissance) Squadron, based at Leuchars in Scotland, and then flying Ansons, and by the outbreak of war in September 1939 the unit was fully equipped and ready for action. Crews found the Hudson had twice the range of the Anson as well as greater speed and bomb load, and its advent was warmly welcomed.

Action soon came, for on the second day of the war one of No. 224's Hudsons patrolling over the North Sea attacked a Dornier 18 twin-engineed flying boat engaged on similar work; in doing so, it became the first RAF aircraft to attack the *Luftwaffe*. In October 1939 two more of Coastal's Anson squadrons, Nos. 220 and 233, converted to Hudsons, and on 10 November a pair of 220's aircraft scored the command's first *Luftwaffe* 'kill' by damaging a Do 18 so badly that it had to alight on the water, after which it capsized. In addition to their regular reconnaissance patrols, Coastal's Hudsons (which began to be fitted with Mk I air-to-surface vessel radar during that first wartime winter) attacked enemy merchant shipping, minesweepers and U-boats.

In February 1940, a No. 233 Squadron Hudson directed naval forces to the German prison ship *Altmark* (an auxiliary of the pocket battleship *Graf Spee*) hiding in a Norwegian fjord and, as a result, many British prisoners of war were set free. That fateful year also saw Hudsons make low level bombing attacks on enemy airfields in Norway and the battle cruiser *Scharnhorst*, give air support to the British Expeditionary Force during the Dunkirk evacuation, and make nuisance raids by night on airfields in Western Europe whence the Luftwaffe's bombers conducted their nocturnal Blitz against Britain.

Meanwhile, following the passing of the Neutrality Act by Congress in September 1939 — an Act which forbade US citizens to deliver arms to European belligerents — Britain became concerned that its supply of Hudsons would be cut off. Lockheed solved the problem by buying an airstrip — near Pembina, North Dakota — which lay jointly in the US and Canada. Until the US eased Neutrality Act provisions, Lockheed pilots flew Hudsons to North Dakota. Horses pulled the aircraft up to the international boundary, whence they were able to pass the border into Canada without violating neutrality laws. Air delivery from Canada began in November 1940; take-off point was the vast airfield at Hatties Camp, Gander, Newfoundland, the 2,700-mile flight usually being made at night. The first trans-Atlantic Hudson ferry flight was made on 10/11 November and involved seven Mk III Hudsons, captain of the lead-ship being Capt D. C. T. Bennett, DSO, of BOAC, later to lead the famous No. 8 Group, RAF Bomber Command — the Path Finder Force — and attain the rank of Air Vice Marshal.

The number of Hudson squadrons grew to five during 1940, and in the following year a further six entered the lists, including four units specialising in anti-shipping work as opposed to the Hudson's normal GR role, which primarily involved shipping *protection* by means of convoy escort and anti-submarine patrol. Bases as scattered as St Eval in Cornwall, Wick in Northern Scotland and Aldergrove in Northern Ireland were used by the Hudson units, and during the second quarter of 1941 No 269 Squadron moved to Iceland to conduct its anti-submarine and convoy escort duties from there. On 27 August 1941, one of 269's Hudson's from Iceland spotted a U-boat and made two sighting

Above: Deliveries of Hudsons to Britain by air began in November 1940. The Hudsons included in this picture, taken in the US in April 1941, were part of a batch of 18 which made what was then stated to be the 'greatest mass delivery in aviation history'.

Left: Hudson flight deck scene eight or nine thousand feet above the Atlantic during a Canada-UK ferry flight.

reports to base before being relieved by another machine of the squadron, flown by Sqn Ldr J. H. Thompson. This Hudson, S-Sugar, came across the sub when she had surfaced 1,200 yd away from smoke floats marking the spot where she had previously submerged, and the Hudson attacked with four depth charges just as she was about to submerge again. The U-boat *(U-570)* was completely enveloped by the explosions and shortly afterwards submerged completely. Two minutes later she shot to the surface and ten or twelve or the crew, wearing yellow life-jackets, appeared on the conning tower and came down on deck. The Hudson dived and opened fire with its machine guns as it swept around the submarine in tight turns. The seamen scrambled below, and seven minutes later the captain's

Above: Hudson III T9465 *Spirit of Lockheed-Vega Employees* was, as its name suggests, a free gift to the RAF from Lockheed. It served with No 269 Squadron, Coastal Command, in Iceland from May 1941, and in mid-1943, after a spell of retirement from active duty, joined No 161 (Special Duties) Squadron at Tempsford, Befordshire, which flew 'cloak-and dagger' missions over enemy-occupied Europe.

Right: Bombs go aboard a 206 Sqn Hudson I in 1940. One of the two fixed, forward firing .303in Browning machine-guns can be seen protruding from the topside of the nose. From Mk III onwards first-line RAF Hudsons often had a retractable ventral gun platform for a single .303in Browning.

Below right: The *U-570* being guarded by a Catalina flying boat after surrendering to a Hudson of No 269 Squadron operating from Iceland in August 1941. *Imperial War Museum*

frilled-fronted white dress shirt was cautiously waved from the conning tower in token of surrender. The Hudson signalled base, and asked for surface craft to take off the German crew. Hudsons and Catalinas maintained a constant guard over the arrival of British vessels, subsequently providing air escort for the *U-570* as it was towed to Iceland. This was the first occasion when a submarine had been captured by an aircraft, and, after revealing her secrets to British technicians, *U-570* was commissioned for service in the Royal Navy as *HMS Graph* — under which name she was soon in action against one of her sister-vessels. Eventually, in March 1944, she was wrecked off the coast of the island of Islay, Scotland.

Above: Hudson Mk V AM753 carrying four 3in rocket projectiles beneath each wing; RP-equipped Hudsons were first used operationally in the Mediterranean theatre.

In Iceland the weather could often be as hostile as the enemy. Freezing gale-force winds — sometimes developing into hurricanes — fog and ten-tenths cloud seemed all too frequent to the boys of Coastal, and on one occasion, when bad weather caused a Hudson to be diverted to an emergency landing ground near the coast, it was ten days before it could take off again. 'During that time', commented a wartime Air Ministry PRO, 'the crew consumed ninety-two tins of meat and vegetable ration and on their return regarded bully beef and biscuits with much the same feelings as the Israelites displayed towards the fleshpots of Egypt.'

Another Hudson squadron became active in Coastal Command in 1942, but the year also saw the start of the phasing-out of the type as a front-line machine, though the command continued to employ it for meteorological duties and, air-sea rescue, for which latter purpose it was sometimes fitted, from 1944 onwards, with a Mk I airborne lifeboat of the type designed by the famous yachtsman Uffa Fox.

1942 was a particularly busy year for the Hudsons. In February they took part in the attack on the *Scharnhorst* and *Gneisenau* during their infamous Channel 'dash' which followed their breakout from Brest, while in May they participated in the attack on the *Prinz Eugen* off Norway. May was the peak month for Hudsons engaged in the mast-height attacks known as *Rovers* against enemy merchantmen and minesweepers, more than 50 vessels being sunk or damaged off the Dutch and Norwegian coasts. June saw 35 of Coastal's Hudsons take part in Bomber Command' third 1,000 bomber raid, against Bremen, on the night of 25/26th, their specific target being the Deschimag U-boat yards, and their weapons being 100lb anti-submarine bombs. No 53 Hudson Squadron flew from St Eval to Naval Air Station Quonset Point, Rhode Island, USA, in July 1942 to co-operate with the US Navy in anti-submarine warfare, later moving south to continue its work from a base in Trinidad for a while.

Throughout the year, Hudsons continued to play a big part in the Battle of the Atlantic and also rescued hundreds of ditched aircrew personnel from the sea. Prior to the Allied invasion of French North Africa — Operation *Torch* — in early November 1942, three UK-based Hudson squadrons were switched to Gibraltar for work in the Mediterranean. November and December 1942 were their peak months of activity, one squadron alone making 37 attacks within a fortnight; on one occasion 11 U-boats were attacked in the space of two hours. It was during these operations that a Hudson of No 500 Squadron, captained by Flg Off M. A.

Ensor, dived from 7,000ft to only 50ft in an attack on a U-boat and scored a direct hit on its magazine or torpedoes. The explosion ripped the sub wide open and simulataneously removed the Hudson's rudders and elevators, damaged the ailerons and bent about 6ft of both wing tips up at right angles. The crew balanced the aircraft by running fore and aft, and Ensor (who had destroyed another U-boat in the previous July whilst operating over the Atlantic) managed to bring it close to friendly territory before being compelled to order the crew to bale out. Unfortunately, two of the crew lost their lives, but Ensor and his rear gunner survived and were rescued by a sloop.

Hudsons continued in first-line use in the Mediterranean theatre until the war's end, some having underwing rocket projectiles added to their armament. They also did much transport work there, a particularly noteworthy episode being the Gibraltar-Malta shuttle service which was officially inaugurated on 10 January 1942 to meet the difficulty of despatching urgent supplies at a time when Malta was under almost continual bombardment by enemy aircraft. On an average, seven Hudsons maintained the service, and due to the prevailing conditions on Malta it was only possible to land and take-off there at night — and, furthermore, to do so only during periods of quiet. The approaching Hudsons were warned by radio when an air raid was in progress, and they had to fly a southerly course and 'stooge' around until the all-clear. Despite this rule, however, the aircraft did on occasions land during a raid because, if a wireless operator happened to be taking his bearing, he did not pick up the air raid signal.

No aircraft were permitted on the airfield during daylight as it was not desired to present enemy aircraft with a sitting target, so the crews barely had time for a hurried meal before taking off again. One pilot recalled landing in Malta 18 times without once seeing the island in daylight. Also no serivicing could be undertaken at Malta and one Hudson actually made a return trip with its main spar shattered by an enemy cannon shell.

Despite these hazards, not one Hudson was lost in the air during the operation. On one occasion two passengers were hit by machine-gun bullets and one of them died subsequently. On another ocasion a Hudson went into a power dive to shake off an attacking Junkers 88 and the ASI showed 380mph — probably a record for a Hudson. Needless to say the engines were changed before the aircraft went up again.

The Hudsons carried an almost endless variety of supplies: Spitfire parts and tyres, wireless sets and spares, small arms ammunition, medical supplies including blood plasma, mails, cigarettes, soap — just to mention a few items. The aircraft never returned to Gibraltar empty and women and children evacuees were carried away to safety. So precious was the aircraft space that maximum load rules often went by the board; as much as possible was crammed in. Between April 1942 and August 1943 the Hudsons on the Gibraltar-Malta shuttle service carried 6,680 passengers and 2,029,000lb of freight. To do this they flew a total of 1,270,000 miles in 9,400 flying hours. Each shuttle averaged 15 hrs duration.

RAF Hudsons also served in the Far East, and during the Burma campaign they helped cover the British retreat, thereafter continuing on reconnaissance, bombing and transport duties (including air-mail carrying) in the area. Supply-dropping was one major facet of their transport work, and as the war in SE Asia progressed a partly Hudson-equipped special duties unit came into being to drop arms and agents to Burmese and Malayan guerilla forces. Hudsons also served in substantial numbers with the RAAF and RNZAF in the Far East and South Pacific was zones, lesser wartime users including the RCAF, SAAF, Chinese Nationalist Air Force and the Portuguese naval air arm. The Chinese had but a single squadron and Lockheed sent a service representative to instruct crews. He found that only one man in the squadron spoke English and that aircraft with hydraulic systems and automatic pilots were a complete novelty to the Chinese. The latter had no hangars, no machine shops, no electrical equipment. But the sturdy Hudsons required little attention. 'We'd crank 'em up day after day,' the service rep later reported, 'and they'd run as sweet as ever.'

Some 490 Hudsons designated AT-28s and AT-29s plus 300 AT-18 navigational and gunnery trainers were supplied to the USAAC/USAAF, while 20 PBO-1 patrol bombers went to the US Navy.

Right: The Strathallan Collection's Hudson IV, which has since been repainted in the markings of No 13 Squadron, RAAF.
John Hunt

ADASTRA AERIAL SURVEYS
VH-AGJ

G-BHAB
Valor
G-BEXZ
Stables
Car Hire
York

Ballooning build-up

The history of hot air ballooning spans almost two centuries, man's first ever flight dating from an ascent by the Marquis d'Arlandes and M. Francois de Rozier in a Montgolfier balloon on 21 November 1783: the intrepid pioneers were airborne for nearly 30min and covered a distance of over five miles across Paris. After periods of intermittant development during the subsequent 180 years, the two decades since 1960 have seen a major revival in hot air ballooning for sporting and commercial purposes, and there has become established a large market and widespread enthusiast following for these elegant and colourful shapes in the sky — some of which are seen here.

Left: Balloons at Marsh Benham, near Newbury, Berks during the 1980 'Icicle Meet': in the foreground is one of the new, single seat, 16,000ft^3 Thunder Skychariots, G-BHAB. *Peter R. March*

Above: The agreeable revival of hot air ballooning nicely expressed on the envelope of the British Gas flame-shaped Colt 56SS balloon, G-BGOO, seen during inflation. *Peter J. Bish*

Right: Hot air balloons come in all sizes as well as shapes; this is a Safferey S330 miniature balloon. *Peter J. Bish*

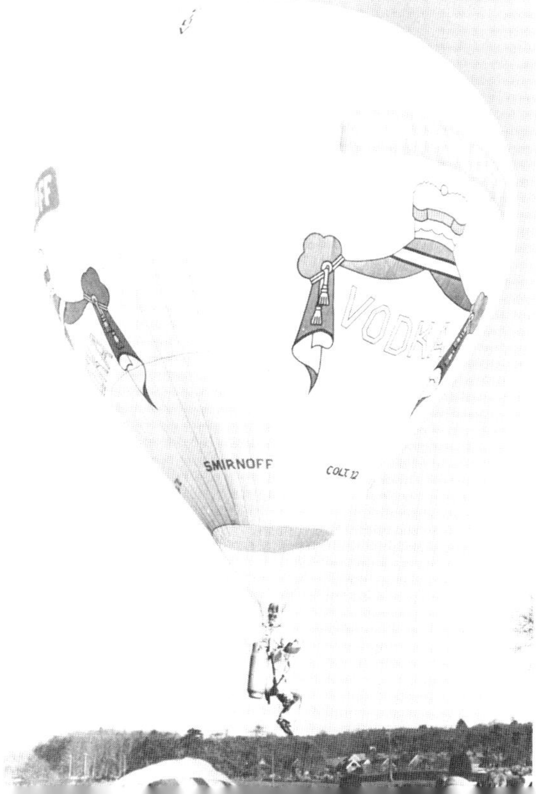

Above left: Finnish-owned Cameron balloon with the humorous registration OH-POP seen during the 'Icicle Meet' at Marsh Benham in January 1980. *Peter R. March*

Above: The number of sponsored aerostats has grown rapidly in recent years as the advertising attractions of hot air balloons have become widely realised. This Thunder Ax8-105 is seen with a hang glider hitching a lift. *Peter J. Bish*

Right: In the superb setting of the Chateau de Balleroy, France, a US-built Barnes balloon sits in tethered stateliness. *Peter J. Bish*

Left: Tiny Colt 12, G-BIDV — literally a single-seater! *Andrew March*

N2008F
F B X U M

American
AA

American's Half-century

John Huizing

For fifty years now the appellation 'American' has been synonymous with the development of the airline industry in the United States. The title first appeared in January 1930 when American Airways Inc was formed by a holding company, the Aviation Corporation (AVCO), to merge the interests of five smaller carriers that had been acquired during the previous year. Routes were redrawn, the previously separate managements of the subsidiaries were re-organised and the aircraft inventories were integrated; and in October 1930 the purchase of another airline — Standard Air Lines — brought with it traffic rights between El Paso, Tx and Los Angeles, Ca thereby allowing the fledgling 'American' to complete a coast-to-coast route from New York to Los Angeles. In May 1934 the original company was succeeded by American Airlines Inc, the name by which the airline has been known ever since.

Left: As befits one of the major airlines in the US, American has played an important role in sponsoring the development of some of the most famous designs produced by that nation's aircraft manufacturers: two of the aircraft — the DC-3 and the DC-10 — are seen here in this commemorative photograph taken at San Diego, Ca in 1971. American was the first airline to take delivery of both aircraft, starting services with the wide-body trijet in August 1971, just 35 years after it had introduced that most famous of all the Douglas Commercial series aircraft to its route network in June 1936.

Inset left: A renowned pioneer of aviation in the US, Charles A. Lindbergh, was associated with one of American's antecedents. On 15 April 1926 Lindbergh stowed a bag of mail in his DH4 biplane of Robertson Aircraft Corp and took off from Chicago for St Louis. The company had been only the second private operator to be awarded an air mail contract by the US Government and it later became one of the many component enterprises which went to form American Airways.

Above right: An early photo of aircraft used by Robertson Aircraft Corp — far left a DH4 mail plane, and two Waco 10s: the one on the right was a training aircraft.

Centre right: One of the airlines acquired by AVCO in the late-1920s was Colonial Air Transport which had won Air Mail Route No 1, New York-Boston in 1926. Colonial operated in the US Northeast and Canada, and in 1929 introduced the 14 seat, trimotor Keystone Patrician, the largest passenger plane of its time.

Bottom: The Pitcairn Mailwing was used until 1933 on mail only services in the Eastern Division of American Airways between Newark, Albany, Cleveland and Boston. The aircraft was powered by a 300hp Wright Whirlwind engine and could cruise at 110mph.

Photographs compiled by **John Huizing**, *and courtesy* **American Airlines Inc**

N9683
N9683
AMERICAN AIRWAYS
U.S. MAIL
Ford
TRI-MOTOR

Above left: Running up its engines before departing from 'Gate No 1' at an unidentified airport in 1928, a Fokker F10 trimotor of Transamerican Airlines Corp, another of the pre-1930 components of what was to become American Airways.

Left: An example of the famous Ford Tri-Motor pictured in 1930 and wearing the title and emblem of the newly formed American Airways. The exact location of the photo is unknown but judging from the names on the railroad bridge (St Louis, Kansas City, Memphis, Birmingham, Pensacola), the size of the river, and the sandbanks, the aircraft is thought to have been over the Mississippi.

Above: The Stinson T was introduced by American Airways in 1931.

Right: The cabin interior of a Ford Tri-Motor — somewhat spartan accommodation but generously sized windows by today's standards.

This picture: 'The plane that changed the world', the Douglas DC-3: it evolved from a wider fuselage version of the DC-2 to accommodate 14 sleeping berths on US transcontinental services and known as the Douglas Sleeper Transport (DST). But it was quickly realised that a day plane version of the aircraft with 21 instead of 14 seats would be a winner and it was this machine, incorporating a series of airframe design, powerplant and other developments, which became the DC-3. American put the DST into service in 1936 and it did indeed work wonders: the year before the airline had made a loss of over $750,000 but by 1938 this had been turned round to a profit of over $200,000, and in 1939 the airline recorded a surplus of $1.4 million.

Bottom left: An American Airways Curtiss Condor photographed in 1934. These 18-seaters served on the American network from that year and later became 15 berth sleepers on the company's circuitous coast-to-coast route.

Top right: Also introduced in 1934 was the Vultee V-1A and by the time of this photograph, as can be seen on the fuselage side, the airline had become American Airlines.

Bottom: The DC-3s later rendered valuable service as freighters, not only with American but with other airlines and armed forces around the world.

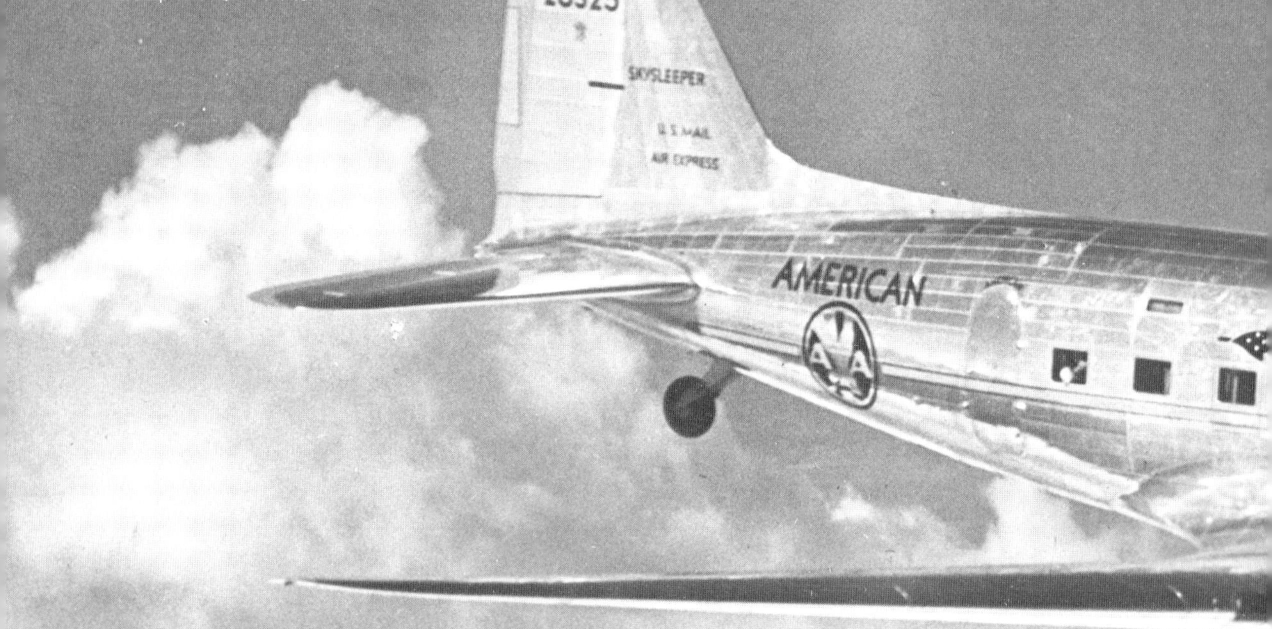

NC13767

aqship Skysleeper

WEZEY
H.E.SWEZEY & S
MOTOR TRANSPORTATION
EASTPORT, L.I. N.Y. PHONE 25
Flagship Airfreighter

Below: The Consolidated Vultee Model 39 Liberator Liner, a development of the US Navy RY-3 (RAF Liberator Mk IX), was used by American Airlines for an experimental air cargo service across the US but the aircraft did not go into production. The availability of numerous ex-military transports at the end of WW2 did not facilitate the introduction of new designs like this.

Bottom: In mid-1945, American Airlines acquired a majority holding in American Export Airlines (AEA) and subsequently formed a subsidiary called American Overseas Airlines (AOA) to manage the interests of its new affiliate. AEA had been operating flying boat services to Europe but in October 1945 these were followed by AOA's start of scheduled landplane services with DC-4s over the Atlantic, American inaugurating these flights ahead of its two US rivals on the trans-Atlantic route — Pan Am and TWA. The photo shows an AOA L-749 Constellation at La Guardia Airport, New York in 1949.

Above: Joining the Constellations on the trans-Atlantic services were Boeing Stratocruisers such as *Flagship Great Britain*, N90941, shown here. American Overseas Airlines' operations lasted until 1950, when the company was sold to Pan Am.

Below: In the late-1940s, American's Douglas-built equipment on US services — DC-3s, DC-4s and DC-6s — was augmented by the Convair Model 240 Convair Liner, the airline being a major customer for the twin-engine, short-to medium-haul airliner. Deliveries started in 1948 and this photo shows NC94219, *Flagship Newark*, flying over Washington DC.

Top: Six years after American's 1953 start to non-stop transcontinental services between New York and Los Angeles, the airline began its jet service on the same route with Boeing 707s. This aircraft is a later version of the airliner, a turbofan engine-powered 320B, N8436, which was delivered in 1969.

Above: Another airliner whose design was largely the result of an American Airlines requirement was the Lockheed Electra, a four turboprop transport that began services with the airline in the same month as the Boeing 707, January 1959. N6102A, *Flagship Chicago*, was the airline's second Electra.

Above: The '400 Astrojet' title denoted the srs 400 version of the BAC One-Eleven ordered by American Airlines in July 1963 for short-haul services

Right: The following year, 1964, saw the start of American's operations with the Boeing 727, destined to become the most widely used type in the airline's inventory during the 1970s with over 140 on strength and further aircraft still to be delivered.

Below right: A vivid impression of the way in which the cabin appearance of air travel has improved during recent years is shown by this view of the first class section on an American Boeing 727 which has been given the wide-body look treatment. It also makes an interesting comparison with the accommodation aboard an earlier generation of three-engined airliner shown in the photo on page 107!

Below: American was among the early operators of the Boeing 747 and although obtaining its first purchased aircraft in mid-1970 only a year after deliveries began to the lead customer (Pan Am), it had leased examples of the type ahead of its first 'official' delivery.

Bottom: American took a leading role in the definition of the wide-body airliner specification which led to Douglas and, later, McDonnell Douglas evolving the design of the DC-10; and the airline placed the first order for 25 (with 25 options) of the large trijets in February 1968. The order was for the US transcontinental version capable of non-stop operations, the DC-10 srs 10. The aircraft first flew on 29 August 1970 and almost exactly a year later (5 August 1971), the DC-10 made its revenue earning debut on American's Los Angeles-Chicago route.

Above right: A wide-body interior proper: a view from the centre of an American Airlines' DC-10 economy class cabin with 8 abreast seating on a twin-aisle arrangement.

Right: Night scene showing a Boeing 747 freighter being loaded with containers.

Freighter
American
SAT4630AA
FMC

WW1 aviation in North East England

J. M. Davis

During peacetime, the presence of military aviation in the North East of England has always been rather inconspicuous. However, the two major conflicts of this century saw military aerodromes sprout up throughout the region, mainly for training purposes between 1939-1945 but of a more operational nature during the Great War.

It was WW1 which brought military flying to the North East and, unlike that in most other parts of the country, it was not confined to the often mundane duties involved in aircrew training. The presence of a relatively large number of operational aerodromes was in part a reflection of the great industrial output of the area. Heavy industry, based on local deposits of coal and iron ore, provided plentiful targets for Zeppelins, while extensive coastal shipping attracted German submarines. The realisation that aeroplanes formed the most effective means of defence against these elusive raiders brought about the formation of units by both the Royal Naval Air Service (RNAS) and the Royal Flying Corps (RFC) in order to provide an adequate aerial defence.

The RNAS was the first to base a unit in the region. On 18 November 1914 the first complete flight of No 1 Squadron was detached from Gosport to Newcastle, equipped with four Bristol TB8s. By 1915, the RNAS had stations at Whitley Bay and Redcar, both of which flew aeroplanes on early anti-Zeppelin patrols. The Tyneside raid by the 'P' type Zeppelin L10, on 15 June 1915, brought an unsuccessful attempt at an interception by an aeroplane from Whitley Bay. Although many unsuccessful patrols were flown from Redcar, the station was primarily concerned with pilot training, and equipped with a variety of machines including Grahame-White Type XVs, Caudron GIIIs, Maurice

Right: The Author's map of WW1 aviation locations and incident sites in the North East of England.

Below: A Short 184 floatplane being beached, reportedly at Seaton Carew. *Frank Yeoman Collection*

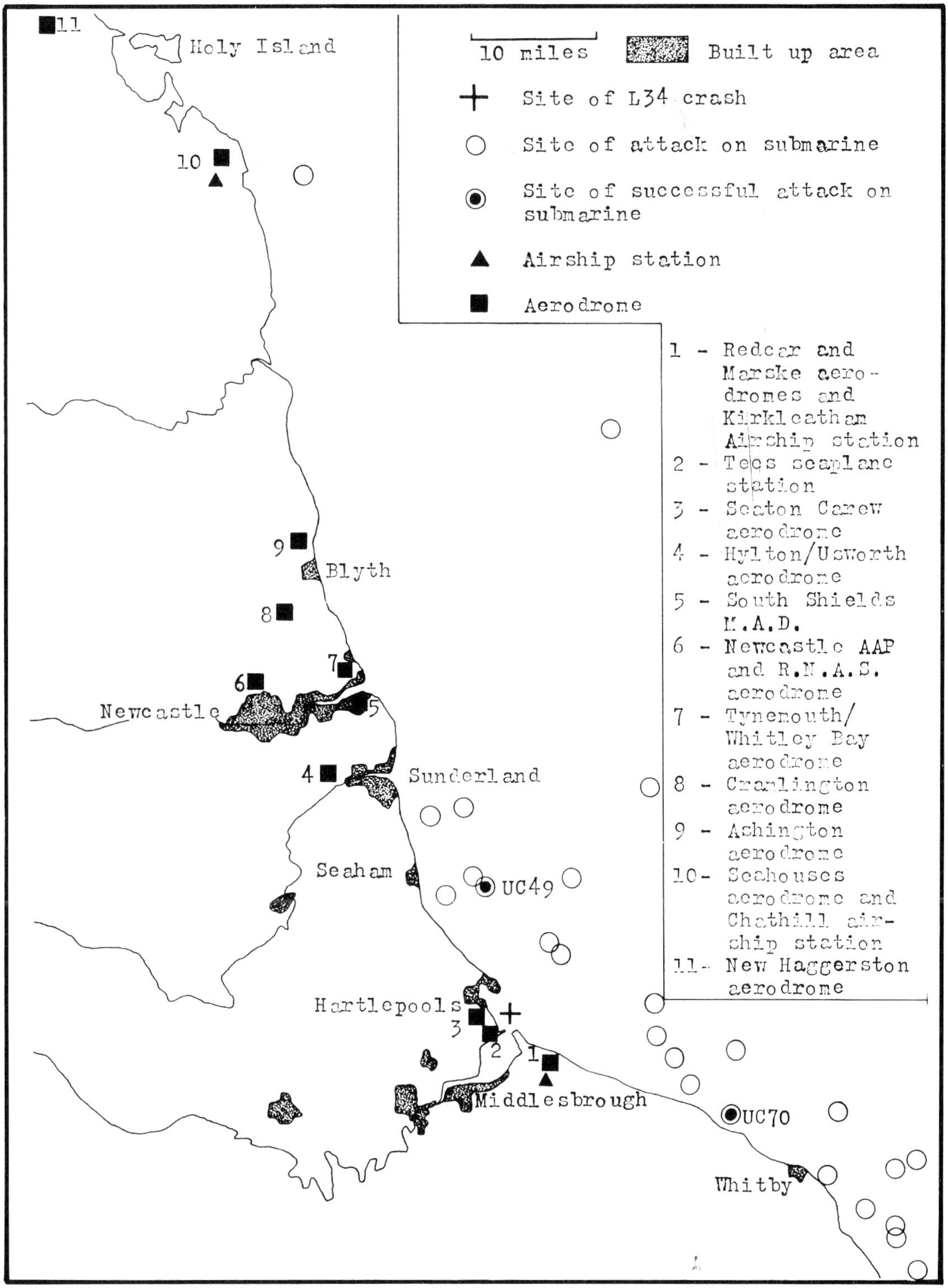

10 miles
Built up area
Site of L34 crash
Site of attack on submarine
Site of successful attack on submarine
Airship station
Aerodrome
1 - Redcar and Marske aerodromes and Kirkleatham Airship station
2 - Tees seaplane station
3 - Seaton Carew aerodrome
4 - Hylton/Usworth aerodrome
5 - South Shields M.A.D.
6 - Newcastle AAP and R.N.A.S. aerodrome
7 - Tynemouth/Whitley Bay aerodrome
8 - Cramlington aerodrome
9 - Ashington aerodrome
10 - Seahouses aerodrome and Chathill airship station
11 - New Haggerston aerodrome
Holy Island
Blyth
Newcastle
Sunderland
Seaham
UC49
Hartlepools
Middlesbrough
UC70
Whitby

Above left: 2-Lt Ian V. Pyott of No 36 Squadron RFC who accounted for Zeppelin L34 shot down into the Sea of Teesmouth during the night of 27 November 1916. *Photo via the Author*

Above: An Armstrong Whitworth FK8, D5139, built by Angus Sanderson & Co at Newcastle. *Photo via the Author*

Farman 'Longhorns' and an assortment of Avro 504 variants. Several of the naval pilots who trained at Redcar were later to achieve fame over the Western Front, the most notable being Raymond Collishaw.

The menace posed by the Zeppelins prompted the RFC to follow the lead taken by its naval counterpart. At Cramlington, three BE2C aeroplanes, which had been used for training, became the initial equipment of No 36 Squadron when it formed on 1 February 1916 under the command of Captain R. O. Abercromby. In May of that year, the squadron's establishment was increased by the addition of FE2Bs and BE12s coinciding with an expansion of its area of operations to include Teesside and the Firth of Forth. In order to provide adequate coverage of these new areas, flights were detached to Seaton Carew, near Hartlepool, and Turnhouse, to the West of Edinburgh. In June 1916, No 58 Squadron came into being at Cramlington, as an offshoot of No 36 Squadron. This new unit flew a variety of training aircraft until, in December 1917, it received a full complement of FE2B machines and flew out to France as a night bombing squadron.

The detachment of a flight of No 36 Squadron to Seaton Carew paid its first dividend on the night of 27 November 1916. Flying a BE2C (serial number 2738) from Seaton, South African born 2-Lt I. V. Pyott shot the Zeppelin L34 into the sea off the mouth of the River Tees. This airship was one of four from a force of eight that has taken off for targets in the North East. L24 was to bomb a benzole plant at Stockton-on-Tees, L36 was intended to attack targets along the Firth of Forth and the other two, L34 and L35, planned to make for Tyneside. L34, flying at just over 9,000ft, was the first to reach the coast, which it crossed at Blackhall's Rocks, to the north of Hartlepool. Almost immediately, a searchlight at Castle Eden illuminated the airship, which dropped 13 small bombs as it swung to the south at the start of a turn to take it back out to sea. Further searchlights tracked the Zeppelin and Pyott, patrolling over Teesside when he sighted the enemy, flew northwards to intercept. Weak anti-aircraft fire has been directed at the airship, so Pyott fired a flare to signal his intention. Searchlights were switched off and the gunfire ceased as he made his initial attack, which was followed by a turn to the east.

The Zeppelin had turned in the same direction so Pyott flew a parallel course, firing short bursts into its port side. A further 16 bombs were dropped by L34 as it passed over West Hartlepool, perhaps in an attempt to gain height and climb away from the attacker. It was too late, however, as Pyott's firing had hit and ignited a gasbag. The airship's fiery fall into the sea took several minutes and was clearly seen by the other Zeppelins, which took immediate action to avoid the area. L35 and L36, to the north, were both suffering from mechanical trouble and so abandoned their missions, their commanders having no intention of sharing the fate of their colleagues on L34. The older L24, some twenty miles from the coast and on a course for Stockton, turned south towards Scarborough, which its commander, Kurt Friemel, later claimed to have bombed. There were no survivors from L34 and the death of its commander, Max Dietrich, was particularly untimely — 27 November 1916 was his 46th birthday. Pyott returned to Seaton Carew at midnight, to become a local hero. Official recognition of his night's work came later, in the form of a DSO.

No 36 Squadron underwent a re-organisation during December 1916. Seaton Carew became its main base, while detachments were made to Hylton (near Sunderland) and Ashington (on the Northumberland coast). In order to increase their efficiency, several of the unit's FE2s were modified to single seat configuration — the observer's position being faired over and a single Lewis gun fixed in a forward firing position, on a level with the pilot's head. The removal of No 36 Squadron's Turnhouse flight had been provided for by the formation of No 77 Squadron at that station during the previous October. Flying the usual assortment of BE2 and BE12 variants, No 77 Squadron had detachments at Penston, Whiteburn and New Haggerston (the last mentioned being in Northumberland, from which the Border region was protected until January 1918).

The destruction of six airships by the Home Defence squadrons during the Autumn of 1916 brought about a massive reduction in airship attacks on this country — there were only seven during 1917 (although aeroplane raids were started against targets in the south). For No 36 Squadron, 1917 was a year of inactivity and so the January 1918 placing at the Admiralty's disposal, for anti-submarine work, of the flights at Seaton Carew and Ashington probably came as a welcome diversion.

Against all expectations, a final Zeppelin raid on the North East did take place, however. The attack was made on 13 March 1918 by L42, under the command of Martin Dietrich. Although recalled after a change in wind direction, Dietrich stood off the Northumberland coast until dark and selected Hartlepool as the target. All of the region's towns were lit up, as no raid warning had been given, and after a long approach from the north, L42 dropped 21 bombs on West Hartlepool before climbing away out to sea. An FE2D was airborne from Seaton Carew, piloted by 2-Lt E. C. Morris with 2-Lt R. D. Linford as his observer. From its patrol height of 15,000ft, the FE was coaxed up to its ceiling, at which it was still below the airship. Although Morris and Linford opened fire, they were out of effective range and were forced to give up the chase after following the Zeppelin for 40 miles out to sea.

With the formation of the RAF in April 1918, Seaton Carew became the region's main anti-submarine base and so No 36 Squadron moved to Usworth (as Hylton became known), where it re-equipped with the Bristol F2B. For the remainder of the war its main role was the training of night fighter pilots. The CO during the latter half of 1918 was Major W. J. Tempest — a name well known in the field of night fighting. With the Armistice, a move was made to Ashington by the bulk of the squadron and disbandment soon followed, on 13 June 1919.

Despite its great industrial reputation, the North East played only a minor role in aeroplane production during the Great War, turning out about 2,500 airframes. The reason for this relatively small output was the nature of the region's industry; aeroplanes of the time were produced mainly by small firms, such as coachmakers (who had experience of working in wood) and not by the heavy industrial giants. Sir W. G. Armstrong, Whitworth and Co Ltd, of Gosforth, and Angus Sanderson and Co, of Newcastle, built several types of aeroplane during WW1 but the majority were FK8s — about 1,500 of which were produced, with manufacture almost evenly shared. The earlier FK3 had been produced by the parent company, after its 51 sub-contracted BE2Cs had proved far from easy to manufacture. In the last year of the war, the two firms each built 250 sub-contracted Bristol F2Bs, in addition to the final batches of the FK8.

The output of the two Tyneside manufacturers, although modest, necessitated the establishment of an acceptance facility, so No 9

Above: Fairey Campania on the sands, reportedly again photographed at Seaton Carew. *Frank Yeoman Collection*

Above right: A Blackburn Kangaroo, B9973, of No 246 Squadron at Seaton Carew in late-1918. This machine was credited with causing slight damage to a U-boat on 30 May 1918. *Photo via the Author*

AAP was opened at Newcastle, on the Town Moor. This was used to check out not only the main production types but also the experimental Frederick Koolhoven designs, such as the FK10 Quadruplane. The preparation of aeroplanes for delivery was also the role of the Marine Acceptance Depot sub-station at South Shields, where flying boats and seaplanes were readied for service. Short 184s seem to have been the main type handled, although the end of the war saw the arrival of Felixstowe F3 and F5 components for assembly. At the same time No 9 AAP had 21 Sopwith Cuckoos on charge, but the massive cancellation of orders brought about by the Armistice removed the need for the acceptance units, which closed during the following year.

The Autumn of 1916 had seen the virtual elimination of the Zeppelin menace, but the following year brought the rise of a new threat when the German Navy began large scale submarine operations. Much of the North East's prosperity depended upon shipping. Ship building and repairing were the main industries along the banks of the region's rivers and much of the Durham and Northumberland coalfield's production was transported by collier to London and other ports of Southern England. All of this shipping offered a multitude of choice targets for German submarines and by the end of 1917 the North East War Channel was one of the two most dangerous areas for British coastal traffic.

The defence of British coastal waters was naturally a task for the RNAS and initially its anti-submarine force comprised SSZ-type 'blimps', based at Chathill, near Seahouses, and at Kirkleatham, near Redcar. These non-rigid airships were only present in small numbers, one or two at each station, and their capabilities left so much to be desired that a flight of four Handley-Page 0/100s of 7(N) Squadron at Coudekerque was detached to Redcar for a month from 5 September 1917. During their detachment the 0/100s sighted eleven submarines, seven of which were attacked, and although there were no sinkings the presence of aeroplanes had the effect of keeping the enemy submerged, which reduced the sighting and attacking of British vessels. In October, the Handley-Pages were moved to Manston to become the initial equipment of Naval 'A' Squadron. This move meant that the North East coast was once again only protected from the air by the SSZ 'blimps'.

In order to make good the deficiency, the RFC placed the Seaton Carew and Ashington

flights of No 36 Squadrons at the disposal of the Admiralty from late-January 1918. As a Home defence unit, No 36 Squadron had been fairly inactive since the end of 1916 and its FE2Bs were easily adapted to anti-submarine work, being capable of carrying two 100lb bombs. The FE2s served in this role until June, when sufficient Blackburn Kangaroos were available at Seaton Carew to patrol the area satisfactorily. When enough floatplanes became available, the RNAS added to the anti-submarine force by opening a seaplane station on the northern shore of the Tees estuary. Known as Tees Station, this base first housed No 452 Flight, equipped with six Sopwith Baby aeroplanes. Later Nos 402 and 403 Flights were added, flying Short 184s and, as it would appear from photographic evidence, at least one Fairey Campania.

Very little change was brought about by the formation of the Royal Air Force on 1 April, although the Tees Station did become attached to the nearby Seaton Carew airfield. Two types of aeroplane were soon introduced to the RAF's anti-submarine operations, the Blackburn Kangaroo and the DH6. Being a twin-engined, three-seat machine capable of carrying up to four of the flat nosed, 230lb anti-submarine bombs, the Kangaroo greatly increased the efficiency of patrols when it entered service with No 495 Flight at Seaton Carew and gradually took over from the FE2s. Eventually, ten of these aeroplanes were based at Seaton and although their operations were plagued by frequent mechanical trouble, they proved to be ideally suited to their task. The DH6 on the other hand, was not intended to be an attack aeroplane — it was, after all, a redundant trainer. If flown as a single seater, it could carry a 100lb bomb but it was usually assigned to the 'Scarecrow' patrols. These were a system whereby aeroplanes flew a regular patrol 'beat', with the intention of keeping submarines submerged and thus relatively harmless. A total of seven DH6 flights were based along the North East coast, from New Haggerston to Seaton Carew.

A rationalisation of units took place during the summer of 1918, when the scattered anti-submarine flights were grouped into squadrons apparently on the basis of aeroplane role. The eventual equipment and disposition of these units was as follows:

No 246 Squadron

402 Flight —	Seaton Carew	Short 184
403 Flight —	Seaton Carew	Short 184
452 Flight —	Seaton Carew	Sopwith Baby
495 Flight —	Seaton Carew	Blackburn Kangaroo

No 252 Squadron

507 Flight —	Tynemouth	DH6
508 Flight —	Tynemouth	DH6
509 Flight —	Seaton Carew	DH6
510 Flight —	Redcar	DH6

No 256 Squadron

525 Flight —	Ashington	DH6
526 Flight —	New Haggerston	DH6
527 Flight —	Seahouses	DH6
528 Flight —	Seahouses	DH6

Between March and September 1918, these units made 31 attacks on submarines. The Kangaroos of No 495 Flight made eleven of these and had the best record, being credited with one confirmed destruction (shared with the Royal Navy) and causing slight damage to at least two enemy vessels. No 452 Flight's Sopwith Babies made a further 11 attacks but only one of these resulted in damage. Of the seven attacks made by the FE2s, two were classified as causing slight damage, although that on UC49 was later confirmed as a destruction. Only two attacks were made by DH6s from Tynemouth, and neither met with any success. Space does not permit a detailed account of every attack that was made on enemy submarines, but a summary of these from March to September 1918 is given in the accompanying table. Three, however, are worth looking at more closely; one because it shows the stringency of claim classification and the other two as they resulted in the destruction of their targets. It should be noted that after the initial aeroplane attack both incidents required the assistance of surface vessels to complete the destruction.

An attack which resulted in the official classification of 'Possibly Slightly Damaged' took place on 27 August 1918. Lt Cooper, on patrol from Seaton Carew in Kangaroo B9978, had already attacked one submarine when another was sighted at 11.50hrs, in a position 13 miles to the south east of Whitby. The aeroplane's remaining 230lb bomb was released and it appeared to explode on the periscope, causing large quantities of oil and air bubbles to rise to the surface, accompanied by a body and a peculiar reddish fluid. Despite these apparently successful results, only the above-mentioned category of claim was allowed.

The first destruction of a submarine in the area had occurred almost three months earlier, with the participation of FE2B A6535 from Seaton Carew. While patrolling at 1,200ft on the morning of 31 May, Lt Beal had sighted a submarine five miles off Seaham, and promptly descended to 300ft before dropping two 100lb bombs on the vessel's clearly visible outline. The first fell ahead of the port bow, the second an estimated seven feet on the starboard beam, and after the subsequent explosions oil and air bubbles appeared on the surface. The destroyer *HMS Locust* was attracted by this activity and proceded to depth charge the area. Although RAF communiques had only claimed 'possible damage', it was later learnt that the submarine, UC49, had been destroyed.

A Blackburn Kangaroo, B9983, took part in the second sinking on 28 August. Piloted by Lt E. F. Waring, with Lt H. J. Smith as its observer, the aeroplane was armed with a single 520lb bomb when a long oil slick was observed off the North Yorkshire coast. The source of this oil proved to be a submarine, which was spotted at 3.25pm, lying in eighty feet of water, on the sea bed off Runswick Bay. The circumstances (date, location, leaking oil and the vessel's stationary nature in such dangerous waters) suggested that this may have been the craft attacked the previous day by Lt Cooper. Smith released the bomb which was seen to explode 30ft from the submarine's bows. Large bubbles of oil and air rose from the enemy vessel and the aeroplane's crew fired flares to attract the attention of surface craft in the vicinity. *HMS Ouse*, a destroyer, arrived to lay a pattern of depth charges, one of which exploded on the submarine's hull to complete its destruction. A subsequent investigation of the wreck by divers showed that the vessel had been the UC70.

After the end of the war, the anti-submarine units were soon dispersed. No 495 Flight was transferred to Seahouses during November 1918, but its stay was brief and a subsequent move to Killingholme was followed shortly by disbandment. The remaining units of No 246 Squadron were disbanded during May 1919 followed on the last day of June by the North East's other two coastal squadrons.

Throughout 1917, Redcar had continued as a centre for the training of Naval pilots, but during the last year of the war it assumed a more interesting role with the formation of No 2 School of Aerial Fighting. This RFC unit was based on the southern part of the Redcar

Above right: A Sopwith Snipe, E8189, of the Fighting School at Marske seen during the winter of 1918-1919. The pilot on the left is Capt G. M. Knocker of No 63 Training Squadron.
Frank Yeoman Collection

Right: A Sunbeam Motor-built Avro 504B, N5264, which crashed while serving at RNAS Redcar in *circa* 1917.
Photo via the Author

120
E8189

aerodrome, which was known as Marske to avoid confusion with the RNAS station. No 2 SAF received prospective scout pilots from the training squadrons, to give instruction in tactics and some experience of live gunnery. Sometimes complete units passed through the School, an example being the United States 25th Aero Squadron, which was attached for training from 25 April until 7 August 1918. The nature of the unit's work necessitated the use of current operational aeroplanes and so No 2 SAF was equipped with a variety of front line machines, which included Camels, Dolphins, SE5s and, later, Snipes. It was, supposedly, while serving with this unit that Capt A. R. Brown, of 209 Squadron fame, broke his neck in a flying accident. Towards the end of 1918, No 2 SAF appears to have been re-titled, to become No 4 Fighting School, although its role remained unchanged.

Until June 1918 the training of flying instructors had been undertaken by the School of Special Flying, but a decentralisation of this work became necessary and one result was the formation of the North Eastern Area Flying Instructor's School at Redcar. In addition to the usual Avro 504Js, the School was also equipped with several Camels. On 6 October 1918, No 63 Squadron began a move from Joyce Green to Redcar; two days being taken to fly up the unit's machines — except for a two seater Camel whose 20min duration necessitated its transportation by road. Capt G. M. Knocker, the Camel Flight commander, was the first to arrive at the new base, landing in his red and white Camel at 08.50hrs on the 8th. Others were less fortunate; two Camels and six Avro 504s crashed on the journey. No 63 TS soon resumed its work, being obliged to turn out a certain quota of pilots each month. The rate of attrition was high, however, and Knocker's personal Camel was an early casualty, being ditched in the North Sea by a pupil named Burns on 22 October. Four days later, a crash involving Sgt Burridge temporarily left the Camel Flight with only one aeroplane!

Above: Albatros DV visiting Redcar while on a tour of RAF aerodromes in October 1918 — in the cockpit was Capt Smith MC. *Frank Yeoman Collection*

Right: Lt Graham of No 63 Training Squadron standing in front of one of that unit's unarmed Sopwith Camels at Redcar in 1919. *Frank Yeoman Collection*

The signing of the Armistice, on 11 November, resulted in an outburst of low flying by the pilots from Redcar. The local beaches were the favourite scenes of these antics, but Knocker outdid most by flying under the Transporter Bridge at Middlesbrough — twice. An unusual machine at Redcar at this time was an Albatros DV, which was on a tour of home airfields and had been flown in by Capt P. F. Fullard, the No 1 Squadron ace.

In common with other units in the region, those at Redcar were disbanded during 1919 and this rapid closure of stations resulted in military aviation vanishing from the North East. It was 11 years before it returned and when that happened only one of the original airfields, Usworth, was re-opened. The other WW1 stations were either too small or too poorly located to be considered for further use, although Cramlington saw some civil flying as the home of the Newcastle Aeroplane Club. The site at Seaton Carew was re-opened as a ground station and remained in use until recently, the underground plotting rooms still existing although the land surface has reverted to farmland. Flying continues at Usworth, which is now Sunderland Airport, but no traces remain of the original airfield. The only remnants of Great War aviation in the region that can be seen today are the seaplane slipway into the Tees Estuary and two of the old sheds at Marske, the latter being used as a store by ICI.

Below: Sopwith Triplane, N5912, of the Fighting School at Marske during the winter of 1918-1919; this is the machine preserved today in the RAF Museum at Hendon.
Frank Yeoman Collection

Aeroplane attacks on submarines of the North East Coast — March to September 1918

Date	*Time*	*Aeroplane & Base*	*Pilot*	*Location*
25.3.18	17.05	Baby N2101 Tees Station	Flt Sub Lt Waring	15m east of Hartlepool
6.4.18	13.15	Baby N2110 Tees Station	Lt Addis	5m east of Sunderland
26.4.18	12.14	FE2B A5542 Seaton Carew	Lt MacDonald	2m south east of Seaham
1.5.18	17.05	Baby N2101 Seaton Carew	Lt Richardson	South east of Sunderland
8.5.18	13.20	FE2B A6586 Seaton Carew	Lt Penny	4m east of Seaham

Representative aeroplanes of units based in North East England 1914-19.

No 1 (N) Sqn detachment: Bristol TB8 —

RNAS Whitley Bay: BE2C — 1099.

RNAS Redcar: Avro 504A — 2929, 2933, 2934.
Avro 504B — 9865, 9866, 9867, N5264, N5266.
Avro 504C — 8600.
BE2C — 1109, 1145.
Bristol Scout C — 1250.
Caudron GIII — 3265
Curtiss JN4 —
Grahame-White Type XV —
Maurice Farman S7 'Longhorn' — N5057

No 36 Sqn: BE2C — 2738
BE12 —
Bristol F2B —
FE2B — A5542, A6535 and A6586 at Seaton Carew.
A5684 and A5738 at Ashington.
FE2D —

No 58 Sqn: BE2C —
Armstrong Whitworth FK3 — A9972.
FE2B —

No 77 Sqn detachment: BE2C —
BE12 —

No 7 (N) Sqn detachment: Handley-Page 0/100 — 3123, 3127, 3131.

No 246 Sqn: Blackburn Kangaroo — B9971, B9972, B9973, B9975, B9976, B9978, B9983.
Fairey Campania —
Short 184 —
Sopwith Baby — N2067, N2101, N2107, N2109, N2110, N2111.

No 252 Sqn: DH6 — B3082, B3090 and C2079 at Tynemouth.

No 256 Sqn: DH6 — C5172, C7336

No 2 SAF/No 4 FS: Armstrong Whitworth FK3 — B9594.
Armstrong Whitworth FK8 — B252.
Bristol F2B — C4695 (76)
Bristol M1C — C5000 (92)
DH4 — B5524
DH5 —
SE5 —
SE5A — D3943 (47).
Sopwith Pup —
Sopwith Triplane — N5912 (94).
Sopwith Camel — B5721, E1456.
Sopwith Dolphin —
Sopwith Snipe — E8189 (120).

NE Area FIS: Avro 504J/K —
Sopwith Camel —

No 63(T) Sqn: Avro 504J/K —
Sopwith Camel — F4187.

Bombs dropped	*Observed result*	*Official classification*	*Remarks*
One 65lb	None	Not Classified	Bomb fell astern
One 65lb	Oil appeared on the surface instantly	?	Destroyer continued the attack and depth charged
One	Some oil rose to the surface	Not Classified	Submarine sinking a vessel when sighted
One 65lb	Numerous bubbles	Not Classified	Aircraft short of fuel so returned to base
One	Much oil rose to the surface	?	Attack followed depth charging by a drifter

Date	*Time*	*Aeroplane & Base*	*Pilot*	*Location*
8.5.18	19.05	FE2B A5542 Seaton Carew	Lt Ainscon	15m east of Redcar
8.5.18	13.35	FE2B A5684 Ashington	Lt Taylor	13m south east of Seaham
10.5.18	?	Baby N2109 Seaton Carew	Lt Richardson	4m south east of Skinningrove
10.5.18	15.47	Kangaroo B9971 Seaton Carew	Lt Waring	7m east of Whitby
30.5.18	07.30	Baby N2111 Seaton Carew	Lt Addis	20m east of Sunderland
30.5.18	07.50	Kangaroo B9973 Seaton Carew	Lt Dean	10m south east of Whitby
31.5.18	09.18	FE2B A6535 Seaton Carew	Lt Beal	5m east of Seaham
31.5.18	12.45	Baby N2111 Seaton Carew	Lt Clutterbuck	12m east of Whitby
31.5.18	?	FE2B A5738 Ashington	Lt Riley	5m east of Beadnell
8.6.18	10.42	Kangaroo B9972 Seaton Carew	Lt Richardson	20m east of Hartlepool
13.6.18	10.35	Kangaroo B9972 Seaton Carew	Lt Richardson	12m east of Seaham
19.6.18	06.40	FE2B A5542 Seaton Carew	Lt Toyne	?
30.6.18	09.55	Baby N2067 Seaton Carew	Lt Addis	20m north east of Scarborough
26.7.18	15.35	Baby N2067 Seaton Carew	Lt Addis	?
27.7.18	16.50	Baby N2107 Seaton Carew	Lt Clutterbuck	1½m south east of Whitby
28.7.18	07.50	Kangaroo B9975 Seaton Carew	Lt Richardson	35m ENE of Hartlepool
28.7.18	?	Kangaroo B9972 Seaton Carew	Lt Dean	12m east of Teesmouth
28.7.18	17.07	Kangaroo B9976 Seaton Carew	Lt Waring	12m south east of Seaham
12.8.18	19.15	Baby N2109 Seaton Carew	Lt Taylor	5m north east of Whitby
17.8.18	08.25	DH6 B3082 Tynemouth	Lt Whitmore	25m east of Druridge Bay
21.8.18	19.50	DH6 C2079 Tynemouth	Lt Gibson	3m south east of Sunderland
27.8.18	07.10	Baby N2109 Seaton Carew	Lt Clutterbuck	9m south east of Whitby
27.8.18	11.35	Kangaroo B9978 Seaton Carew	Lt Cooper	6m south east of Whitby
27.8.18	11.50	Kangaroo B9978 Seaton Carew	Lt Cooper	13m south east of Whitby
28.8.18	15.25	Kangaroo B9983 Seaton Carew	Lt Waring	Runswick Bay
3.9.18	12.55	Kangaroo B9975 Seaton Carew	Lt Richardson	10m east of Redcar

Bombs dropped	*Observed result*	*Official classification*	*Remarks*
One	Patches of oil on the surface	Not Classified	—
One	?	?	—
One 65lb	None	?	Patrol of area continued by Baby N2107
Two 230lb	None	?	Bombs fell ten yd on either side of submarine
One 65lb	Small patch of oil	Not Classified	Bomb fell four yd from conning tower
Two 230lb	Some oil rose to the surface	Possibly Slightly Damaged	Bombs exploded ahead of the periscope's wash
Two 100lb	Oil and bubbles of air rose to surface	Possibly Slightly Damaged	*HMS Locust* depth charged to destroy UC49
One 65lb	Small quantity of oil on the surface	Possibly Slightly Damaged	Bomb fell six yd from starboard bow
Two	Oil and bubbles of air	Possibly Slightly Damaged	One bomb seen to explode on edge of conning tower
Two 230lb	Oil and bubbles in great quantities	Not Classified	Bombs dropped from 1,000ft. *HMS Cicala* continued patrol
One 230lb	Oil and bubbles of air	Not Classified	Drifter continued the attack with depth charges
Two	Bubbles and a thick patch of oil	Not Classified	The aeroplane was on a convoy patrol
One 65lb	None	Not Classified	Bomb failed to explode. Aircraft on convoy escort
One	?	Not Classified	Attack made on one of two submarines in that area
One	None	Not Classified	Submarine had just sank a vessel off Whitby
Two	None	Not Classified	Bombs failed to explode. Area searched by RN
Two	?	Not Classified	Aeroplane's attention attracted by a trawler
Two 230lb	?	Not Classified	One bomb appeared to hit conning tower
One 65lb	None	Not Classified	Bomb fell short
One 100lb	None	Not Classified	Search taken over by DH6 B3090 but submarine lost
One	None	NotClassified	Attack continued by RN but no positive result
One 65lb	None	Not Classified	Area later depth charged by two Motor Launches
One 230lb	Great quantity of oil and bubbles	?	Bomb exploded 40ft from the periscope
One 230lb	Oil, bubbles, a body and some red fluid	Possibly Slightly Damaged	Bomb appeared to explode on periscope
One 520lb	Large bubbles of Oil and air	Known Destroyed	Attack completed by *HMS Ouse* with depth charges
Two 230lb	Oil and bubbles of air	Not Classified	Bombs dropped at one minute interval

About:
AIRCRAFT ILLUSTRATED

This Annual bears the same name, and is produced by the same editorial team, as the popular monthly magazine. *Aircraft Illustrated* features all the latest aviation news plus articles on military and civil aviation, all supplemented by the very best in aircraft photography. If this Annual interests you, so will the magazine. It is available through newsagents or on subscription from the publisher, IAN ALLAN LIMITED, Subscriptions Department, Terminal House, Shepperton TW17 8AS.

Below: The roll-out of the BAC 221 at Filton Bristol: the aircraft was a rebuild of the first prototype Fairey FD2 designed to test the unusual delta wing that was to be used on Concorde. As well as a revised wing the '221' also featured a lengthened fuselage and taller undercarriage. *British Aircraft Corporation*